*The* Devil's
Dozen

# The Devil's Dozen

THIRTEEN BULGARIAN
WOMEN POETS

*Translated by Brenda Walker with Belin Tonchev
in collaboration with Svetoslav Piperov*

FOREST
BOOKS
London & Boston

SVYAT
Sofia

PUBLISHED BY

FOREST BOOKS
20 Forest View, Chingford, London E4 7AY, UK
61 Lincoln Road, Wayland, MA 01778, USA

& SVYAT PUBLISHERS
11 Slaveikov Sq, 1000 Sofia, Bulgaria

Typeset by Svyat, Sofia
Printed by Svayt, Sofia

All rights reserved. No part of this publication may be reproduced, stored in a retrieval system, or transmitted, in any form, or by any means, electronic, mechanical photocopying, recording or otherwise, without the prior permission of the publisher.

*British Library Cataloguing in Publication Data*
*The Devil's Dozen.*
1. Poetry in Bulgarian, 1990 – Anthologies
891.811308

*Library of Congress Catalogue Card No:*
90–71089

ISBN 0–948259–84–1

# Contents

INTRODUCTION by Milena Tsaneva ... xi

DORA GABÉ
   \*\*\* The flower in the pot on my window sill ... 3
   Possessions ... 4
   \*\*\* Life why do you hurry ... 6
   At Peace ... 7
   \*\*\* Sea, why are you writhing ... 8
   \*\*\* There is no empty space ... 9
   Remain quiet ... 10
   Incredible ... 11
   Freedom ... 12
   Silence ... 13
   Question ... 14
   Transient ... 15
   Will ... 16
   Last testament ... 17

ELISSAVETA BAGRYANA
   A cry ... 21
   Snow ... 22
   The elements ... 23
   The cuckoo ... 24
   Descendent ... 25
   My song ... 26
   Rendevous ... 27
   S.O.S. ... 28
   Dreams in the garret ... 30
   Hands ... 32
   The Well ... 33
   Fire-dancer's destiny ... 36
   Comet ... 37

BLAGA DIMITROVA
Strength 41
Introduction to the Beyond 42
Midnight bell 43
Heroics 44
Grass 45
Self portrait 46
A bird's lot 48
Chinese Wall 51
Touch 53
Eagles are vanishing 54
Bach's harmony 56
Dispute about poetry 57
Frost 58

LYUDMILA ISSAEVA
Don't let the world grow old 61
Blue blood 62
Poems of others 63
In Memoriam 64
Grocery 65
A dove's feather 67
Love 68
Recollection 69

LIANA DASKALOVA
Love in Thrace 73
Shrovetide 75
*** I shall set you free 76
Defencelessness 77
Comb 78
That's how it should be 79
So far I have kept dumb 81
This life 82

## LILYANA STEFANOVA
Talent 87
When I feel sad 89
\*\*\* Nothing could be scarier 91
\*\*\* Our souls are together 92
The bracelet 93
An empty sky 94
A blue streak in the sky 95

## STANKA PENCHEVA
Advice to myself 99
Planets 100
A monologue by Eve 101
The great game 102
Declaration of love 103
Belated experiment 105
The circus is leaving 106
Something like an auto-epitaph 107
The season of losses 108

## NADYA KEHLIBAREVA
Heiress 111
A page from an old book 112
Breaking point 113
A bright patch 114
Omen 115
Things not said 116

## EKATERINA YOSSIFOVA
If only I hadn't been so distracted 119
\*\*\* You said: I want us to do something together 121
Granny 122
The mirror 123
Work 124
\*\*\* I suspect 125
Sirius 126
\*\*\* It's your fair I'm going to 127
Earth 128

RADA ALEXANDROVA
   Summer     131
   Voices     133
   At night     134
   *** In the garden three yellow stalks grow     135
   Where     136
   *** Have mercy on us     137
   *** This cup did not pass from us     138
   *** From out of memory     139

KALINA KOVACHEVA
   *** They say: He's far away     143
   *** While I'm away wasting ripe moments     144
   *** He said: You talk to gods     145
   *** And words never obey me     146
   *** Disasters enveloped me     147
   *** The woman with the string-bag     148
   *** It was Someone – midnight     149
   *** He makes safe his door     150
   *** A happy man never writes poetry     151

MIRYANA BASHEVA
   *** Behind the thorn-crowned forehead     155
   *** Scientific yet accessible     156
   *** My foolish, evil star fades     157
   The eighth of December     158
   Business     159
   You, we and I     160
   Birthday     161
   The wolf cub     162

VANYA PETKOVA
   Strength     165
   Summer     166
   By the North Sea     167
   How good it is     169
   Full of you     171
   Sinner     172
   Calling     173
   At my father's grave     174

# Acknowledgements

The publishers would like to thank Stanka Pencheva for compiling the book and writing the poets' biographies. We are particularly indebted to Svetoslav Piperov for his dedicated work on the literary translation of the poems. Our thanks are due also to Vladaimir Levchev for his help with the translation of Blaga Dimitrova's poems and to Lily Netsova for the translation of the introduction and biographies.

# The Dance
# of the Fire-walkers

The thirteen women poets in this collection present the colour and nuances which women's varied views and experiences bring to modern Bulgarian poetry.
For many years poetry in Bulgaria was considered the domain of men. The first modern Bulgarian poets emerged last century during the growing struggle for national liberation. They were primarily national leaders and figureheads, such as Hristo Botev who was shot in 1876 while leader of a revolutionary detachment. He marked the beginning of a heroic literary tradition which turned Bulgaria into a "land of martyred poets".

This accounts for the relatively late emergence of women poets. There were sporadic attempts at female writing before the country's liberation from Ottoman domination in 1878. These were mostly in the prevailing patriotic spirit. Women poets with their own style did not appear until the first decade of the 20th century. At that time Bulgarian poetry had already shifted from the evils of society to personal problems. After the First World War, in the vital post-war atmosphere, the verses of the young Elissaveta Bagryana raised a defiant voice against centuries-old prejudices and opened the doors to unrestricted female influence in Bulgarian poetry. Her first volume, *Vechnata i Svyatata* (The Eternal and the Sacred) was published in 1927 and was followed by the debuts of a new generation of Bulgarian women poets during the late 1920s and early 1930s. The pioneering first two "feminine" poetic waves (Maria Belcheva, Ekaterina Nencheva, Dora Gabé, Elissaveta Bagryana, Blenika, Magda Petkanova, Maria Groubeshlieva) seemed to be in a hurry to reveal different philosophical and psychological dimensions of individual femininity.

From the 1930s and especially after the Second World War, women assumed more prominence in Bulgarian poetry and became naturally integrated into their literary generation and existing trends. But they retained a distinctive female voice which transcended set structures. This applies to all 13 women poets included in this collection, who all have individual approaches to the genre.

With the exception of Dora Gabé and Elissaveta Bagryana, whose literary careers are phenomenally long, the poets were born

*Introduction*

in the 1920s, 30s or 40s. They represent the three "middle" generations of modern Bulgarian poetry.

The first two generations experienced the ecstasies and disappointments of society's great revolutionary transformations. The third generation women poets stepped in as already sceptical and aloof members of society. The best works of all these women poets reflect social problems from an intimately human angle while continuing the great national tradition of social commitment.

Women's social status and moral and psychological problems are tackled by several generations of women poets; from Elissaveta Bagryana to Blaga Dimitrova and Stanka Pencheva. They range from defiance of social restrictions to analysis of the new difficulties facing the emancipated "lone woman on the road". The feminine poetic principle guiding all generations since the beginning of this century lies in the perception of reality, the philosophy of life, the peculiarities of the mind, moral concepts and artistic sensitivity.

Despite the differences between literary generations, trends and individual traits, and the specificities of classical or free verse, Bulgarian women's poetry shares some common elements. These include the vitality and willingness to accept life as joy in spite of its hardships and sorrows; the determination to establish harmony even when it is painfully clear that it is lacking in the modern world; the devotion to the values of human life; the delicate sensitivity to the fine points of reality, the meaning of detail; the instinctive attraction to nature; the sensuality which can obliterate the borderline between the animate and inanimate world; and the emotional defiance of old age.

The stoicism of this poetic world has been morally and aesthetically rationalised and is deeply rooted in the national character. The metaphorical self-determination of the woman and the poet in Elissaveta Bagryana's poem *(Nestinarska Sudba)* Fire-Dancer's Destiny comes from national traditions. This poetic metaphor is based on fire-walking, one of the oldest national rituals which is still practised in southeast Bulgaria.

Women's existence and inner life have been changed by social development and this changes the way they are interpreted by

*Introduction*

women poets. They have begun to conceal their vulnerable feminine sensitivity with defiant boyish gestures. The emotional poetic element is being gradually replaced by competent intellectual principles. In the most recent generation of women poets some critics even speak of an apparent "change of roles". Whether she is wearing a romantic dress or jeans and a jacket, the woman poet continues to perform her fire-walker's dance using the hot embers of life to transform every bush into an ever-burning poetic fire. Although this dance may not be part of other nations' folklore, metaphorically it is danced all over the world. The messages of these 13 Bulgarian women poets will reach the hearts and minds of our English-speaking readers.

Milena Tsaneva
*Kliment Ohridski University*
*Sofia, 1990*

# Dora Gabé
# (1888–1983)

Dora Gabé was born on her father's farm near the village of Dubovik in the Dobroudja Plain in northeast Bulgaria. She studied French language and literature at the universities of Geneva and Grenoble. She became founder and president of the Bulgarian PEN Club and in that capacity attended many international writers' forums.Ced poets into Bulgarian.
    Her literary career was unique: after her first poetry book *Temenougi* (Violets) in 1908 she stopped writing for 15 years. After that Gabé wrote mostly for children. Her volume of poetry *Pochakai, Sluntsé!* (Sun, Wait!) was published when she was 79 and changed her image as a poet. It revealed an unsuspected poetic talent. During her final years Dora Gabé wrote her best poems – *Nevidimi Ochi* (Invisible Eyes), *Glubini* (Depths) and *Svetut e Taina* (The World is a Secret). She had a talent for keeping up with the times, speaking the language of all generations, dressing and thinking like them, while having a timeless quality of merging with the elements, with infinity and eternity.

*Dora Gabé*

*Dora Gabé*

\* \* \*

The flower in the pot on my window sill
half opened small white crowns
and said, 'Good morning!'
A ray sneaked through the thin curtain
and slid across my face.
'Get up,' it spoke, 'your writing desk awaits you.'
'I write upon my knee,' I replied.
'Write where you will,
but don't lie a-bed.'
'All right then, I'll get up.'

How wonderful that this world
is peopled with things
and not only with human-beings!

*Dora Gabe*

# Possessions

Dear possessions,
you ask me for nothing
because you know you'll outlive me
and so feel pity...

I'm conscious of you watching
from every corner
carefully reading my face
as I open an envelope
to see if the letter has upset me.

I'm aware of your kindly glance
when I arrive home tired
and fling the mask from my face,
when I wipe off the smile
and take off the jewellery –
And when I sit at my desk
you stay quiet
So I can discover within myself
those old tales and songs
which can turn into a smile!

Sometimes I have left you
because I'm attracted
by distance and high skies,
but when I return
I see how in my absence
grief has covered you with dust,
and veiled your face.

*Dora Gabé*

Dear possessions!
How joyfully we greet each other
when you light up
as I polish you
when we converse silently
every evening,
without ever thinking
that one day
I may no longer return
and you will still be waiting, waiting.....

Dora Gabé

\* \* \*

> *Accept me, Sea,*
> *douse my wounds!*
> Lucian

Life why do you hurry,
why do you outpace me
leaving me alone?
I never carried the yoke of wealth
on my shoulders,
with faltering steps.
I gave away my heart in fragments
so I'd be lighter,
I stretched my homeland into the skies
to lose myself.
Where to stop –
that place where I belong!
Where is the end –
to catch up with it!

*Dora Gabé*

## At Peace

The smallest wave
is dashing towards the shore
having overtaken
all its companions.
Come!
Pass down to me those glances
of the planets who
watched you on your way
and the moon's love songs
with which they quenched your thirst
and the longings
of young sailors
for home, wife and children!
Come!

Spill into my loneliness
into its infinite void!
Alas...
You spill into the sand,
disappear and are no more....

What is 'no more'?
What is 'void'?
'Nothingness,' what's that?
And you, you, who are you?
Why did you leave
so many questions within me?

*Dora Gabe*

\* \* \*

Sea, why are you writhing,
what mutiny
rises from your depths
that you cannot silence?
What fate has caught up with you too,
what misfortune roams the world
which you cannot tolerate?
Lower your voice,
don't frighten away the children
don't drive away
the tiny fish nestling at your breast,
they are not to blame,
so let just me join in
like a howling she-wolf
who has lost her
abducted young...

*Dora Gabé*

\* \* \*

There is no empty space
left in my life,
for you to flood
with your rising tide —
There is no deserted living cell
for death to steal into
unexpectedly.
Together we have passed through storms,
disasters,
the salvation,
and have lived through fear
side by side.
Now lead me into your depths
to the whales
and tiny organisms
so I shall not recall with them
the hour of my birth
and shall not see approaching
the hour of my end...

*Dora Gabé*

# Remain Quiet

Remain quiet,
breathe,
hold within you
that noise of the live wave,
with its tones and sounds,
hold human speech!

Remain quiet
not to miss
the slightest movement
that touches your ear,
or the speck of light
which flies into your eye.

Remain quiet
to listen to the silence
revealing the secrets
of its essence!

Remain quiet
when your thoughts
step upon the earth!

Remain quiet and listen,
listen and remain quiet!

*Dora Gabé*

# Incredible

Like a school of tiny fish
my memories flash
then disappear.
When lightning cuts through
memory
and thunderbolts come crashing –
they never hear.
When real life
catches the intangible
by the wings
they never see.
Even when
the unattainable
collapses on its knees
they don't believe.

But if the rising sun
shines on them
and turns fear
into a tame bird,
they startle,
strain to hear,
and sorrow.....

*Dora Gabe*

# Freedom

It's perched on a twig and is singing.
It's singing freely, filling the air with song,
a song absorbed by the whole of creation.
Who could challenge the freedom
of the wind to snatch the song
and disperse it?
Or the heavy ladened cherry tree
with its blossoming fruit
when it draws sap into its veins –
Who could prevent it from
seeping into the fruit
freely to the rhythm of the song?
I listen, listen and listen
and nothing bars the freedom
of my thoughts from soaring
or even from stealing into
the home of my foe
to beg a brotherly kiss –
I listen, listen and listen
and my free-will grows within me
to love
to rage
and to rush
with outstretched arms
even into the flames.

*Dora Gabé*

# Silence

I don't remember your words —
I remember only your silence
and the room
filled with our thoughts.

I don't remember your features —
they are lost
in my memory,
but I do remember feeling
you were there,
in the large armchair,
and behind you — the window,
the Balkan mountains,
the distant skies
and a small cloud floating by ...

You were the first to speak:
— Why so quiet?
I answered
— I'm not quiet!
You looked at me then smiled
and the sunset glow from the window
bathed our faces in light!

Silence,
a silence overflowing
with love, tenderness and trust!

If we had always spent our lives
in silence
words would never have dared
part us...

*Dora Gabé*

# Question

I'm overflowing
with horror and ecstasy,
love and hatred!
Oh, age of the genius of barbarity
and of man befriended by the stars!
Can I fit
this amplitude
from the lowliest
to the most sublime
into a single soul?
Can I solve
the insoluble issues
of this infinite world?
I envy the sparrow
perched on the bare tree
because it believes
that this world
is just the bough
to the horizon...

*Dora Gabé*

# Transient

With your help
I planted a birch.
The leaves were little hearts
watching
the moon and sun
chasing
never to catch each other.
The birch screened
a small cloud in the sky
and I shaded your
face.

A fleeting moment!

It left its imprint
on the screen
of my memory.
Sometimes I'd project it
onto the sky,
somewhere in the stratosphere...

When night weighs down upon you
and you stare from the window
do you ever catch sight of it?

Water my birch,
for you promised, you know!

Dora Gabé

# Will

You, my loneliness,
my second mother,
From whom are you guarding me?
Bolting
all the doors
and filling out the folds
of the curtain,
lest, God forbid, a sparrow
might spy inside!

Who could be a greater enemy
than the one within
who continually pesters
reproaching me for my faults
and gnawing with bitter words
spoken only by myself
to friends as well as to strangers?!

Let the world enter my home!
For it's not my enemy!
And let me rush into it everywhere!
Let me burn up
so there'll be nothing left for death
when it stops at my threshold!

*Dora Gabé*

## Last Testament

All my life
I've been looking for the man
and have walked past him
without realising it....
I leave it now to you,
Creator of the future —
If you can't find him
create him.

I'll soon be leaving with my thirst unquenched
with eyes still searching the distance,
with outstretched arms
which in my final hour
they'll force into a cross
upon me...

You'll have to be quick,
take me with you,
let me live in your young souls,
don't let my spirit fly
between heaven and earth
so that like an eternal voyager
in its earthly orbit
it will see
without ever being able
to touch....

# Elissaveta Bagryana
(1893–1991)

Elissaveta Bagryana was born in Sofia, the eldest of seven children. Her father was a civil servant from Sliven. She studied Slav languages and literature at Sofia University and taught in a village school for several years which greatly influenced her literary development. The intonations of Bulgarian folk songs and the lively rhythm of popular speech became a salient feature of her poetry. Her first volume *Vechnata i Svyatata* (The Eternal and the Sacred) was published in 1927 and immediately received high critical acclaim. Since then the name of Elissaveta Bagryana has been synonymous with first-class poetry. The works which followed revealed her to be a poet in constant search of new subjects and new means of expression. Elissaveta Bagryana was the first Bulgarian woman writer to speak out naturally and openly about the impulses of the woman's soul, about her unquenchable passion for travel and freedom, and for destroying philistine taboos, deep-rooted morals and spurious ethics. Her poetry is a combination of national and universal values and is so varied that it defies categorisation. The most characteristic motifs are: the four elements; movement as travel, change and protest; love and freedom as synonyms; and the Bulgarian woman's typical stoicism in the face of difficulties. Bagryana's works are much loved at home and have been translated into more than 25 languages.

*Elissaveta Bagryana*

*Elissaveta Bagryana*

# A Cry

In this room, dark and low, not very wide,
I'm dying of an incurable injury
for I am no one's lover, and no one's friend
and there's no one to wait or call for me.

And love was the only thing I ever wanted,
some clear sparkling wine is what I crave for;
by now my venomous thoughts are all recanted
and I pass my enemy with no sign of rancour.

I want to give freely and always be generous
with what hovers inside me, sings and burns,
and have lavish feasts where I swing sonorous
chandeliers madly above welcome guests.

For my youth, aflame and burning fiercely,
and my soul, a skylark of mirth,
and my heart, pulsing full of life and free -
still lift me like a whirlwind above the earth.

*Elissaveta Bagryana*

# Snow

This white winter of fantasy,
a white nameless tale from days of old,
will remain forever in memory
neither written, nor even told.

This odd town I vaguely recall loving
with turrets and gable-roofed eaves,
where lamp-lights budded in the evening
with pale motionless flames.

And the endless streets laced
with long branches and shadows.
And we, taking those first steps —
that took us from rest and sleep...

Black days will follow white
stamped with a seal that's inevitable,
what we lived for in the past,
today we'll no doubt trample.

But there'll come a night one Christmas
when two shadows from our memory
will set out with two unconscious
sighs on a long journey.

And they will stop in this town and pass
into the shining ancient church,
to hold a requiem mass
for our long vanquished youth.

*Elissaveta Bagryana*

## The Elements

Who can hold back the wind which gusts across the hill-tops,
whirls through ravines, lifts dust-clouds high in the air,
snatches the eaves from houses, and the covering from carts,
fells gates, fences and the children on the square
of my home town?

Who can hold back the Bistritsa, that comes seething down in
spring,
breaking up the ice and the supports of the bridges,
that dark, mischievous torrent flowing from its bed
sweeping away the livestock, gardens and small houses
of my home town?

Who can hold back the wine once it's started to ferment
in huge barrels set into bricks that breathe out its odours,
carved in Cyrillic are the words, black grapes, and white,
in cold stone cellars bequeathed by the ancestors
of my home town?

Who can hold me back, disobedient wanderer, lover of freedom,
sister to the wind, the water and the wine,
for whom the unattainable, the infinite is seduction
who always dreams of roads, unreached, uncrossed, unseen.
Who can hold me back?

*Elissaveta Bagryana*

# The Cuckoo

Walking, watching, seeming deranged,
dissipating days and nights in vain.
You say you've grown out of god's world.
don't you see, can't you understand?
I've told you many times before:
Herbs and magic are of no avail,
let them say whatever they will —
I shall never build a nest,
or rear you many pink-cheeked children,
or around the hearth do household chores.
As if born of a sorceress
I feel fated to a life of woe. —
I need to wander about the world,
I need fairs, dances, and courting —
to listen to others without ever tiring
and join in the chorus with everyone else.
My eyes never tire of looking.
my ears never tire of listening.
I never finish laundering silken yarn,
I'm forever snuffing a half-burnt out fire...
And so I shall spend my life like this,
Unsatisified, unfulfilled.
And after I've died, alone, abroad,
I'll turn into a cuckoo-tramp.

*Elissaveta Bagryana*

# Descendent

*To Mania M.*

There are no portraits of ancestors,
nor any family book in my clan
and I'm unaware of their legacies,
their faces, souls, lives.

But I sense the pulsing inside
of ancient, rebellious wanderer's blood.
It stirs me angrily from my sleep
and leads me back to original sin.

Perhaps a dark-eyed grandmother
in silken shalwars and turban,
has run away in the depths of the night
with a foreign light-haired khan.

Perhaps in Danubian plains
they heard the horses' clatter
and the wind that erased their traces
saved them both from the dagger.

Perhaps that's the reason I love
plains too vast for the eye,
horses under a cracking whip,
free voices poured into the wind.

Perhaps I am sinful and cunning,
perhaps halfway I'll break —
But I am your faithful daughter,
Motherland with same blood as mine.

*Elissaveta Bagryana*

# My Song

*To V. Vassilev*

Row me, Boatman, in your light bark,
which noiselessly cleaves resin-black waves
as if breaking a trail from here to the sky,
as if playing tag with free, fearless gulls.

When we're out of the bay, into open sea,
and salty drops spray onto our lips,
and the south wind fills the hoisted sails,
and the white, bewitched boat embarks on its way —

Then, Boatman, I shall start to sing,
an unheard song — about my small motherland,
whose name hangs like a cloud above me,
whose song to me is like honey and wine!

Dark-eyed lasses sing at harvest time,
lads join the chorus and surprise them at evening,
the song is at weddings, late night worker-bees,
and such a song might be mothers wailing.

Never before have you heard this subdued and sinister song,
and perhaps it is only here one can hear it sung,
for no other nation's had such pain for so long,
or suffered more, while dumb and uncomplaining.

Here the snow on mountain tops never melts in summer,
the sea is small, but its name means — blackness,
Vitosha's peak is black, forever fretting and angry,
soil, black and fertile, yet with infinite sadness.

Row me, Boatman, in your light bark,
which fears not foaming resin-black waves,
let us break an endless trail on them —
let's reach the sky and the fearless, free gulls!

*Elissaveta Bagryana*

# Rendevous

I discovered your footprints in the sand and to get there sooner
I ran, legs sinking to the knees, and I fell from exhaustion,
and when I climbed the hill – in astonishment I was calling,
as if I'd seen you for the first time on that unforgettable evening:

You filled the entire horizon, so big you seemed,
with feet on the shore, hair in the clouds.
And you saw me and reached for me –
as if you hoped to embrace the universe – everything...

Listen to my heartbeat, see the tears in my eyes
and remember – no one has ever embraced me like this,
nor have I embraced anyone ever – like this.

And if at this moment my joy lowers the scales
and God wants to shorten the thread of my days,
I shall extend my arm to Him asking for supreme grace.

Elissaveta Bagryana

# S. O. S

In this age of concrete, machines, and the wireless,
of tremendous destruction and of mad searching,
of chaos and of an unclear tomorrow,

in this country — a threshold between East and West,
a vortex of wars and disasters,
where people live for a crust of bread and a small patch of land,

what are our useless lyrics, brothers?
— Homeless dogs' mournful howls to the moon...

Like this one night we'll expire cursed
swept away by the automatic broom of dawn,
when the early-morning cocks wake villages and towns...

But is it our fault we were born not yesterday, or tomorrow but
                                                                   today,
not under Western blue mercurious lights,
not under the exotic rays of the Tropic of Cancer —
but here, where all the winds fill our sails
and where banners of different hues criss-cross each other?

Is it our fault that in our Balkan blood swim
white atoms of Slavonic sentimentalism
and the red — of primitive Tartar tribes?

You see: we dream of the million-ton transatlantic ships
and of oceans in full flood.
          We respect
the hundred-storey skyscrapers of New York.
We dream under the song of aeroplane propellers,
we dance in the rhythms of running engines,
we speak with inspiration before open transmitters —
and go to sleep under the reassuring 'O. K.'
coming from the colonies of Australia...

*Elissaveta Bagryana*

But in our mouths we still sense the taste of the wild hunt
and the fragrance of forest honey.
Our souls open during the warm nights of haymaking,
our emptied hearts still feel the pain of lost love,
when —bumping along the rough mountain road,
under the huge July stars,
among the fireflies and singing crickets
and the scent of ripened field grass –
we are on our way to rustling Balkan woods,
to the downtrodden village wattle fence,
to pour our fatigue into the quiet family home
and our sorrow onto mother's warm breast...

So that's why I say: – I shall die content and with peace of mind
if I manage, being a woman and a poet,
to reveal my heart to the world, as little
as the tiny yellow canary in the cage
above my head in the restaurant,
during the break, when the jazz band takes a rest!...

*Elissaveta Bagryana*

## Dreams in the Garret

Tonight my thoughts soar like a fiery comet
    in interstellar space.
Tonight my longing embraces earth like the Milky Way.
    Oh, this poetic ascension,
    this lyrical intoxication,
    this insatiability of the soul!

Why did you give me this body and this boundless spirit, God?
    This thirst for all seas,
    this hunger for the five continents,
    this heart for every human race
                   for enemy or brother.

Where and how can I escape from my skin —
    I, a vestal, a fury and a virgin,
    I, a poor daughter of Eve?
Shall I always, like the snail, carry the shell of my lot
                   on my back?...

Will I never see the white northern lights,
fly over the tropics or the Atlantic?
Will I never set foot on the islands of Oceania
or my eyes penetrate the southern stars of the Pacific?

Why can't I just go into the travel agents',
    where the multi-coloured map of the world
    hangs stretched on the wall
    like the hide of a skinned panther,
and raising my hand calmly, with self-confidence,
draw an endless curve with my little pen,
saying: — I'll have a ticket for that cruise! —
    And set off on the first express...

*Elissaveta Bagryana*

But I'm no American billionaire, some colonial planter,
gold-digger, swindler, or forger.
       I'm not an English tourist,
       a sailor or an airman,
       nor a famous actress,
       a 'star', or even a 'Miss'...

They say there's a divine spark in me,
but I know my urge will mean my end:
       I shall live like any homeless Bohemian
       who dreams of writing a great poem,
       and yield up my soul like any Bulgarian poet
       bequeathing: to the landlady an unpaid rent,
       to friends – a subscription and some small loan,
       and to future generations – an inspired line or two,
my unappeased hunger and thirst
and the philosophical question: why was man born?

You, who understand and love me,
when I die, don't lament or praise me,
just let the map of the globe be my final bed,
and the star-map my shroud,
       then write:
       Rest in peace between earth and sky,
       poor poet.

*Elissaveta Bagryana*

# Hands

Look at these hands — with their translucent skin,
with their fine web of veins so tenderly blue, —
these soft hands, warm and magnetic — adored,
covered with whisper and burning desires,
bearing so many warm, throbbing hearts —
as though miraculous hands of an ancient icon
(coated in silver by past generations,
enshrining in them life, faith, and future).

I've seen them open up — like lilies to the sun,
then droop, like twigs broken by the storm,
they knew what tiredness was, and hard sweat,
they knew the ladened dish and life's ripe fruit,
the warm, sacred mother-embrace of related blood,
and the awesome sense of ice-cold when touching the beloved
dead...

These hands once held invisible mysteries,
and on them they'd put rings of love —
slim fingers tying fiery knots,
as though mystical links, unearthly — burning.
These were the hands from whose trembling chains
none sought to escape, or grieved for freedom lost...

There they lie, folded now, so indifferent in traquillity,
so indifferent, lonely and empty,
empty of evil and good, of joy and sorrow,
And so they'll go — lonely, helpless, empty
to where no one ever takes anything.

*Elissaveta Bagryana*

# The Well

The heart of my little green oasis
is my well, hidden in the yard
among three birches
and twin pines.
In December the well is warm,
in July, cold,
wrapped in white dawn
and soft evening shadow.
On the bottom,
within the frame of stone,
its water a round mirror.

When I lift the heavy lid
at noon,
the sun comes from the zenith,
across its sky flies a bird,
and into it stormy south winds spill blossom.
When I open it up at night,
I see – a wandering cloud,
the moon throws its platinum discus
a star leaves like an innocent tear,
and the fathomless oval
gleams in full light.

Oh, my dear well,
deep
and clean,
and alive.
Its silence throngs
with human steps.
It's absorbed with lament and laughter,
favourite voices
and children's happy cries.

*Elissaveta Bagryana*

When I am lost
I lean over it
searching for my image in the depths —
and I always find myself again —
in winter frost,
in sweltering heat...

But can you imagine
how difficult it was to grind
through those layers of stone
and hardened clay?
Before one vein of water could find its way,
a huge mound of earth lay
piled upon the ground.

Passers-by stopped
and wondered,
friends asked,
strangers asked:
— What on earth do you need a well for,
now you have a tap in the yard?

I answered,
as if I were to blame:
— To remind me
of the well in Sliven
and of my first flights of fancy,
and the push of that first wave...

—Poetry — they smiled ironically.

But the draught sucked dry
the lakes in summer,
the fountains and the tap water —

*Elissaveta Bagryana*

and people started
to peep into the well,
to draw
its clear water.

Then came a severe winter.
Everywhere froze
and there were
burst water pipes,
but the well
was not seized by the frost.
It breathed out warm vapour
from its depth —
at the bottom
the water was alive
just like
the well at Sliven,
from which I sipped
my first faith.

Elissaveta Bagryana

## Fire-dancer's Destiny*

*To Dora Gabé*

At your fateful crossroads
you've stood for ages, Motherland,
lashed by every wind,
scorched by countless fires.

What secret energy
in your earth and firmament
helped you survive tirelessly
from the holocausts of the past?

Alone and bloodstained,
amidst thistle and nettles,
you gave birth to leaders on the enslaved land
like Ivailo and the Bogomils.

Then you taught your daughters,
deep in Stranja's thicket,
to walk barefoot on glowing embers,
a match for their cruel lot...

And doesn't this dark atavistic gift,
even until recent summers,
explain our women's eternal fate —
to dance on glowing embers?

---

* Fire-dancing is the ancient Bulgarian Nestinari custom.

Elissaveta Bagryana

# Comet

*In 1910 Halley's comet appeared, seen
from the Earth every 76 years.*

In the deep
sky of Sliven, it rose
like an omen with a taut fiery trail.
And all around me grew strange,
turned to air and mother-of-pearl,
most ordinary things like:
our old home,
the sagging eaves,
bolted gates,
the wall with sun-dried loam...

How I waited for you to rise each dusk,
hidden in the dark of my father's yard!
Having just shaken off childhood,
such a visible horizon attracted
where, night after night,
you sank paler,
thinner...

You were my first great wonder,
first mystery of the inaccessible,
unknown, unearthly,
there in the small ancient town, you roused within me
yearning for the powerful,
passion for the eternal.

I know, as a rare guest to our planet,
you'll not rise again for me —
like the heart's greatest passion,
like buried happiness —
once only.

*Elissaveta Bagryana*

Yet all along the restless course of my life,
even in recent days
now melting rapidly
away,
you always left behind an unseen,
yet blazing trace.

# Blaga Dimitrova
## (1922 – )

Blaga Dimitrova was born in the small town of Byala Slatina and brought up in the picturesque town of Veliko Turnovo, a former capital of Bulgaria. She studied Slav literature and language at Sofia University and attended the Moscow Institute of Literature as a postgraduate student. She has a doctorate. She translates Polish, German, French, Swedish and Ancient Greek poetry into Bulgarian. Her poetry and prose have been published in Belgium, the USA, England, West Germany, the Soviet Union, Poland and Hungary. During the Vietnam war Blaga Dimitrova visited the country several times and wrote two books dedicated to it. She has attended many world peace and solidarity congresses. In Bulgaria Blaga Dimitrova is known as a prominent fighter for democracy and human rights.

Blaga Dimitrova has written some 20 poetry books, plus five novels, plays and film scripts. She is a poet who makes no moral compromises, who is never afraid to fathom her own soul. Her poetry is categorical and highly intellectual. Blaga Dimitrova's poems provoke questions even when there are no answers.

*Blaga Dimitrova*

*Blaga Dimitrova*

# Strength

I'm stronger as I am.
I have nothing that can be taken from me,
nothing of mine that makes me tremble in fear,
nothing to lock away in silence.
I don't watch furtively in case of theft.
I can stand fearless facing
the winds of the world.
Come on winds, lash out at me!
What more can you take from me
I've no burden of my own to carry,
so you won't be able to deform me.
I beg to keep nothing personally
so you won't force me to my knees.
I hold nothing in my cupped hands
so you won't be able to shackle me.

I'm free now,
with unfettered wings and thoughts,
so I'm able to embrace everything.
The more you take from me, world,
the more I possess you.
And you'll belong to me
more than ever before, world,
when I stop possessing myself.

*Blaga Dimitrova*

# Introduction to the Beyond

Expiring fully conscious,
you mustered enormous strength
to die peacefully,
without any cry, or moan, or shiver —
so I'd have no fear.

Carefully, your hand
grew cold in my hand
and imperceivably led me
into that beyond to death
just to introduce me.

In the past, and as carefully,
you used to hold my small hand
and lead me through the world,
show me life —
so I wouldn't be afraid.

I'll follow you
with the trust of a child
to that silent country
where you went first,
so I wouldn't feel strange there,

And I won't be afraid.

*Blaga Dimitrova*

# Midnight Bell

*An aural hallucination
Sound-ghost...*
    Boris Pasternak

It's night again. And an even more
uncertain uncertainty.
Sleep runs away from the eyelids
            as if stung.

You wait, listening alertly.
Smoothing the bedding
again and again,
            as you did your husband's grave.

And just when everyone's asleep,
you rend the clean sheeting
of silence with a hoarse shriek:
            — Who's ringing the bell?

And shivering you half open.
Framed in the doorway standing
full length on the threshold
            is darkness.

For a moment you stare at each other
just stare, point-blank. Dumbfounded.
As if you knew one another.
            but from where?

A rapidly slammed door.
A frightened whisper: — It's no one!
The noise of slippers coming back.
            Another stepping on them.

Then for a long time, all by yourself,
amazed, staring into the emptiness
you ask out loud:
            Who rang the bell?

43

*Blaga Dimitrova*

## Heroics

*To some intellectuals et al*

I'd lose all confidence in the future,
if I didn't know people who'd lost their future.

They could, but they don't want to get rich –
grasping their innocent poverty parsimoniously.
They could, but they don't want to win fame –
they're proud enough having chosen to be a nobody.
They could – with hardly any effort –
but don't want to climb upwards.
They've taken the road –what a feat!
Downwards, downwards – to the peak of the root.
And on from there to discover the hidden prospect
of blossom and fruit –still at the pre-embryo stage.

Nameless naive ones who have lost their future–
without you I'd lose all confidence in the future.

*Blaga Dimitrova*

## Grass

    I'm not afraid
they'll stamp me flat.
    Grass stamped flat
soon becomes a path.

*Blaga Dimitrova*

# Self Portrait

So you want to be an icon
 with an iconoclastic image.

Eyes, short-sighted for things near under your nose,
 staring at things in the distance
 which cannot be seen.
Lips with a nondescript shape,
 thirsty, cracked,
 without knowing why.
A smile, resembling a grimace of anguish,
 an anguish, resembling
 a smile.
Gestures like somebody drowning.
 You feel your neck closing in on you,
 and your fingers opening out.
A carelessly free gait, always against the wind,
 creating your own
 cross-wind.
Belongings — countless numbers of lost umbrellas
 and a couple of words
 found minus their armour.

An untidy house, suitcases ready for a journey.
 An uncertain itinerary,
 a certainty in change.
A mind, that doubts the obvious,
 having blind faith
 in the improbable.
Loneliness when at the age of love,
 love when at the age
 of loneliness.

*Blaga Dimitrova*

A shoulder, standing on end, ready to butt
 the closed door
 of the air.
Hands, which let go of everything
 in order to catch hold
 of the wind's beard.

Now travelling lady, what's your mainstay?
 The stumbling-block, perhaps.

*Blaga Dimitrova*

# A Bird's Lot

Pseudo free bird!
Since first memory
you've yielded blindly
to the tyranny of song
(just in case it was considered song).
It has seized you by the throat,
worried life out of you through your teeth.
It drives you out
against the wind's command,
under the guillotine of the rain.
It throws your nest and world
into disorder.
A millstone round your gullet —
your talisman.

        You pseudo bird of God!
        Singing the way you do
      the song only makes you cry.
           It darkens
         your brightest day,
         turning your black
          feathers white.
         Your perkiness —
         to dust and ashes.
      Your aggressiveness —
        to soot and rime.
        your enthusiasm
       to dirt and fumes.

*Blaga Dimitrova*

Pseudo migrating bird!
Do you hope to escape further south
from your shivering with cold?
Here is your fiery south.
Don't fool yourself:
you don't patch up your song,
the song patches you up,
weaving noose after noose,
suddenly after suddenly,
mouth shut after mouth shut,
the cage of your life
(just in case it was considered life).
Are you tapping on the window
waiting for crumbs of love?

        Pseudo song! Pseudo innocent!
        A thorn in the eyes of the blind –
        mafi of philistines.
        A position on a sawn-off branch.
        A flight into fall.
        A challenge to the wind.
        A sting on the heel of Achilles.
        A singing sleeplessness,
        while everything is sleeping.
        A naked cry: 'The King is naked!'
        Insane assault with the sabre of a beak
        A cherry-tree cannon,
        twit! tweet! twit!
        Feathery nitwit finery.

*Blaga Dimitrova*

Pseudo Firebird!
Many live in fear
that you may set the forest alight
with a sun-dipped feather.
The song of the stone in the sling
will betray you.
(A yellow-beaked mob lie in wait.)
You can't atone with a stone!
Turn to the cloud —
it promises a storm:
What armour!

*Blaga Dimitrova*

# Chinese Wall

I recognised it at first sight, and it — me.
Step after step
straight upwards
along the thousand-year-old toothed wall.
I didn't need a guide
or a language for misunderstandings.
Gropingly, I was lead by the umbilical
protocord.

    I was curious through embrasures of loop-holes.
    Beyond,
    as if the same, innocent grass
    and mountain and forest and sky,
    yet entirely different:
    alien, forbidden, dangerous —
    haunts of horrors.
    The wall had marked
    the ridge of fear.

For a long time, I walked the back of this stegosaurus,
rising from horizon to horizon,
from epoch to epoch,
shutting out the air,
crossing out the landscape,
stopping the echo.
Only time like a grass-snake
wriggles, unhindered through it
second by second,
spasm by spasm
century by century.

Blaga Dimitrova

I patted the stones intimately
and spoke to it silently:
You were embedded in my cells
long before I was born.
Your embrasures
are my eyes to the world,
half-closed with suspicion.
Your walls are cemented
with my blood, sweat and tears
stone upon stone,
fear upon fear,
silence upon silence.

How many millennia of eternity will I need
to tear you down within me?

*Blaga Dimitrova*

## Touch

Everything is divided up with a limit line,
which is a contact to something else.

The stem is imprisoned in bark—
through it it feels both wind and rain.

The fish is armoured with scales —
through them it senses the sound of waves.

The sea is clamped by shores —
through them it touches the thirsty land.

I am nailed within a woman's skin —
through it I know caress and wound.

We contact the world
only through our boundaries.

And in becoming more boundless,
we will become more lonely.

*Blaga Dimitrova*

## Eagles Are Vanishing

*With the extinction of animals
something human also vanishes forever.*

The last imperial eagle
has circled for the last time.

He felt a taste of parting in his beak.
What unsolved secrets
did he tie into a faint knot?
What rooted him out of the sky?
Was it lack of air
to breathe and spread his wings?

At dawn who will create
those high outlines of freedom?
Who will continue those flowing circles?
Who will first foresee in the distance
the pirate sails of a hurricane?
Whose eye will be faster than the lightning?
Who will stir the reed's flute
with the beat of wings?

Who with one swing will open infinity
above the towers of crags,
into the eye of the well?

Who will show youth
how to fly against the wind or in no wind?
Who will pierce
the cold breast of the rocks with his claws
to feel the cohesion of the planet?

Who will send me a brave feather
from the clouds plucked out by a storm?

*Blaga Dimitrova*

The last imperial eagle
has circled for the last time.

The azure's smile has frozen
above the rocks and rocked hard.
The comparison 'like an eagle'
has lost all meaning.

*Blaga Dimitrova*

## Bach's Harmony

Bach gave equal rights to every kind of voice
and no voice was allowed to be inferior,
having to serve as an accompaniment or background,
in order that a privileged voice might excel.

And therefore, through the ages, shall go on sounding
that pure, supreme harmony, welding together
free, independent varied voices
into a prayer-like, sovereign unity of spirit.

*Blaga Dimitrova*

# Dispute About Poetry

We were sitting on the shore of the day – two poets, engulfed in a dispute about what is real poetry, and myself who listened to them in silence.

"Poetry," one of them insisted without a shadow of doubt, "that's simplicity. At long last we've got to pull it out of the whirlpools of intricacy!"

"On the contrary!" retorted the other, equally convinced, "Poetry is entangled in the mud-banks of elementalism. We have to drag it to the depths of intricate thinking!"

The dispute was lashing first against one shore and then against the other getting foamier and foamier.

A dragon-fly began to circle between the two, its fine wings carried the faint smile of its last sun-eyed day, then darted straight for the evening.

The dragon fly was neither simplicity nor intricacy.

It was poetry.

*Blaga Dimitrova*

## Frost

*To Todor Borov*

The arrested day is peeping
through bars of frost.

No sparrow dares fly over
the barbed wire of the air.

And the sobbing throat of water
is stopped up with a lump of ice.

And our steps in the snow
are clanging with chains.

For us, there is only one possible escape
from the white prison of winter:

to be our own freedom.

# Lyudmila Issaeva
(1926–1991)

Lyudmila Issaeva was born in the town of Provadia. She has published only two poetry volumes. Her verses convey very personal confessions. One of her poems, *Sinya Kruv* (Royal Blood), provides the key to her style, which is highly noble, full of female pride and sophisticated superiority. Issaeva's heroine is unprotected, vulnerable and yet strong with her inborn sense of dignity. She is rarely confused; moral imperatives are her protection. Her love is girlishly romantic without destructive passions; it is the touchstone of spirituality. In her loneliness she relies on pride and nobility, on "royal blood".

"Don't let the world grow old!" she pleads.

*Lyudmila Issaeva*

*Lyudmila Issaeva*

# Don't Let the World Grow Old

Oh God, can this be maturity? —
To judge the world with a definite gesture
and hand out pious profundity
from the strict pulpit of wisdom...

To weigh virtue in gramms
on righteous scales,
and judge severely others' wrongs,
hiding your own hypocrisy...

And condescendingly to watch the flight
of the children's kite above you,
because you've realised that the kite
will discover nothing at all up there...

Oh, and if that's maturity
don't let the world grow old.
Forgive it even the naivete
of living on illusions...

So let the world have doubts, and err
and chase the clouds and the winds,
let it feel sorrow for children's kites,
and be imperfect or whatever it likes...
When we shall be no more. Then, too.
Don't let the world grow old!

*Lyudmila Issaeva*

## Blue Blood

You hit me!... I felt the pain,
but resisted hitting you back...
Ever since I was born
I've been heading towards this noble art...

It would have been so easy
to ward off a blow with another...
But this is not my price
and my values are above this...

I realised you had strong fists —
All right then, gloat over your gift...
But I pass you by with contempt —
showing how blue my blood is...

*Lyudmila Issaeva*

## Poems of Others

In the night! – Like an escape, a salvation
from petty everyday trials,
when every moment belongs to me
and I belong to myself,

in the hour of weary contemplation,
slowly, as in a solemn hall
I enter – silent, and in awe –
into another's poetic world.

Someone invisibly takes my hand,
and a door opens before me –
And all that before seemed invisible
now takes on meaning and clarity.

Poetry! – a magic alloy
of bewitching colour and sound;
simple words plaited together,
as necessary as daily bread –

into your spheres of wisdom
I enter as before an altar
and bless the mysterious gift
of someone more skilled than I.

*Lyudmila Issaeva*

## In Memoriam

Oh mother! –
I've seen nothing of great hardships
and I've nothing to give me solace...
They say – a good angel descended from Paradise
and took away your righteous soul.

Now at ease, there's nothing more to hurt you.
Your kind smile has reappeared.
And the only thing that could disturb you
is that your hands aren't used to rest.

Over there, you worry that holidays are numerous,
and so, while others are fast asleep,
you hasten to water the star flower-beds,
and sweep out the Milky Way...

At night, when I grieve most,
I gaze long at the skies in mourning
but when they brighten, I know – my mother
has lit the float-light of the moon.

*Lyudmila Issaeva*

## Grocery

Your soul...
I've waited
long and patiently for its locked door
to open before me.
I stepped forward...
and was nailed with amazement –
a well-ordered grocery store
welcomed me.
I caught the whiff
of immaculate order:
the feelings' counter
the obligations' counter,
the disappointments' counter
and a waste bin
for burned out emotions,
needless memories,
experienced moments...
Silently I handed over
the golden coin of my heart.

Like a connoisseur
you felt the weight on your palm.
Then smiled contentedly –
not false.
The shining grocer's scales
weighed out
precisely, diligently
love for one coin.

*Lyudmila Issaeva*

Neither more,
nor less.
Love for a coin.
Diligently.
Precisely.
Suddenly I felt stifled...
Slammed the shop door
and the spring day
lifted me up
in its uncalculating hands...

*Lyudmila Issaeva*

# A Dove's Feather

A peace. A sadness. Birds fly...
On my lapel – a dove's feather.
Because you looked deep into my eyes
I expect no good to come of it.

Something powerful, commanding, surges within me –
how shall I ever endure it?
I'd rather die than let you see
this telltale tearlet.

I see your dark head resting
on my swarthy knees...
Once I believed in such things
but not these days...

Why not? What for? – Better not to ask, don't ask...
Accept me with my dove's feather.
And yet, it's sad that when you look into my eyes
I expect no good to come of it.

*Lyudmila Issaeva*

# Love

...Now, I wonder what I could wish on you,
my dear? —
sleepless nights?
A cheerless lonely room
and unpleasant memories?

But that's not enough... I want
to see a concealed tear roam
in your dark eyes
showing terminal pain.

You, a voluntary captive
in the prison of endless days,
to forget what joy is
and the warmth of the sun's rays.

That is how I'll punish you
for all my bitter sorrows
and for that death sentence
you passed on me...

Yet, I hardly recognize this me,
strange and changeable as I feel,
because your pain
               now makes me happy.

And I thought I was so charitable.

*Lyudmila Issaeva*

## Recollection

...It was too late to save our love —
I was neither your dear or your beloved...
You sauntered slowly over my verses
and disappeared from view.

But in your absence fires broke out —
my meadows and forests set ablaze...
The thunder of evil struck my heart
and the sun shone no more.

And I watched with a face like stone —
how gasping birds dropped to earth
and branched with outstretched arms,
begged mercy from the skies.

But there was no mercy, there was none...
I walked through desolate fields of stubble,
leading me to hell,
and possessed nothing.

...That was long ago... May God save your soul!
And I wonder — what did you do wrong? —
you only sauntered
through my verses and disappeared...

# Liana Daskalova
# (1927 – )

Liana Daskalova was born in Peroushtitsa, a town known for the local population's active involvement in Bulgaria's struggle for freedom during the 19th century. Her first poems often portrayed the homeland and motherhood as part of duty and sacrifice. Nature is another key element of her poetry, not simply as a background but a full-blooded presence. Liana Daskalova is one of Bulgaria's most subtly feminine poets. Her love poems are especially graceful and illuminated. She has published several collections of long poems and almost thirty volumes of poetry.

This book contains poems written in recent years. They are more serious; their colouring seems to have been dimmed by the smoke of autumn fires. They convey restrained sadness and loneliness. She has finished with singing, dancing and celebrating. Pain and loneliness breed the "New, violent manner of writing".

*Liana Daskalova*

*Liana Daskalova*

## Love in Thrace

Orange dress, brown arms —
A girl glowing like a ripe pear!
A wondrous girl with a wondrous face,
Locks like a mane, neck like a dove.

She weaves through the vines
Fiery as a refrain from the south,
swinging to the rhythms of the hora
with her long hair falling free.

Orange dress, swarthy skin,
and a voice that coos like a turtle dove.
Where else can one find such beauty
except here in Thrace.

It was for this that hostile hordes
once swooped over Thracian plains,
to abduct those proud tanned girls
on their black Arab steeds.

For this they'd draw knives, fire pistols
in my Perushtitsa and in Chirpan,
for the right to clasp the thin waists
of those serpent charmers, breakers of hearts!

It was not the wine that started the brawl,
nor the brandy, may it thrice be damned —
those dark-eyed, wild Thracian lads
killed each other for love.

Maiden, maiden with your southern face,
in orange dress, ripe as a pear,
you walk as gracefully as a fiddler
who listens to the sound as he draws the bow.

Liana Daskalova

Slowly you walk, slowly. Surely Beauty
is the most solemn procession of all!
And there by the corner a boy awaits you
among the leaves of horse-chestnut trees.

His forlorn gesture stays you as you pass,
How long each night he's waited in the dark!
So bestow on him a smile lest he should die.
For in Thrace they still will die for love.

*Liana Daskalova*

# Shrovetide

Mercy for those unloved
and for those who remain unwanted,
for the unbefriended,
and for the loveless.
Mercy for the children – the undesired ones,
for those knifed with insults.
Mercy for those without shelter
and
for the wealthy in hushed, lonely houses.
Mercy for the guilty
and mercy for the innocent – for now
it is their turn to sin.
Mercy for mankind,
mercy for the unhappy ones
and for those who are happy!
Now it is their turn to be unhappy.
Mercy for the dead – and compassion for the living.
Mercy for thoughts spoken in anger
and for those thoughts swallowed like the stones of the cherry.
Mercy among all men. Mercy when sat at table.
Mercy – a moon swinging in a blue abyss
like a white khalva on a string at Shrovetide
while the eyes of stars shine with forgiveness.
At least let us show some mercy
and kindness both to the dead and to the living...

*Liana Daskalova*

\* \* \*

I shall set you free, Soul. You can go.
Go on leave me, leave!
I've tormented you enough with earthly woe,
lowly as grass of the field,

I've degraded you with daily routine
that even on a starlit night
you began to feel ill at ease
because of your power of flight.

To this fate, I've brought you down
my dear firebird soul:
instead of being a proud queen
you've become a submissive slave.

So I'll uncover you, set you free
soul with blackened embers,
you're God's gift to me—
no one asked me to pay, to buy you,

Body of Christ, received the wrong way,
sacrificed day after day
just for the sake of daily bread
I placed you in a cage.

I'm aware of the only absolution
for such an unpardonable deficiency:
I sacrifice you not for a feast,
but out of duty, maternal duty...

*Liana Daskalova*

## Defencelessness

We know everything about each other,
I'm sure of that: man is penetrable.
From the strongest feeling our lips betray
one secret thought, one covert joy,
breakable, crystal of vibrating veins
through which a blue sorrow shines...
We are transparent: there good glimmers.
Real glass where evil shimmers,
Gaze, go on, gaze searchingly
at thy neighbour's brow, look intently,
for it is written in a clear style:
Fragile!
And so defenceless and helpless man seems to me
unriddled as far back as memory
his childhood roots, pierced, torn
in the heart of the secret, in the innermost dream,
hollowed out and unravelled strand by strand,
with a soul, twitching like a fish on the sand.
No hidden shadow, no bank to hide under,
you can read man's eyes like a child's primer
and you feel so sorry for this unriddled
creature, for this deity dethroned.
that you slowly offer a compassionate palm
to lay on a humiliated brow, to calm
those betraying eyes. A palm like a veil laid upon
how otherwise could you preserve the prodigy of man?!

*Liana Daskalova*

# Comb

An antique comb, a silver one,
an orphan,
What dark sorrow
in a gleaming comb!

Gone are the hairs fragrant
with olive and oleander.
It no longer reflects
the flame of Palissander.

Not a breath, or sign...
of that hand, so graceful, so fine.
Frayed beauty
left in a comb...

I do my hair, night swims deeply
in the mirror — emerald.
The comb kisses me,
the kiss of Judas,

its teeth rapacious, glistening
in the mouth of Time.
Unsatiated! I see myself fraying
in its fangs,

I see myself unprotected, mortal,
languishing, languishing.
Then no me — a mirror-like abyss.
Left of me — one precious thing

inherited and handed down
from one childhood to another...

*Liana Daskalova*

## That's How It Should Be

I'm getting used to sitting alone.
Not in comfort, not leaning back
in one of those Swedish
deerskin chairs,
not relaxed, but on a hardbacked chair.
      Simple as salt,
      Tough as a peasant.
      Back straight.
      Pure in spirit.
      Sat all alone
      choosing sternly
      rare, rare guests.
I look intently, analyse.
And analysing, see in them
      many faults!
      Sat all alone
      as in a tower,
      waiting, on edge.

Deeply hurt. Chained like a circle, into a nought
      a being alone,
peaked sharp as a Gothic tower,
      one I once saw
bleak, black above white Spring
      in a Swedish town.
      Gothic is
really not my style, makes me drunk,
      that northern style
      floors me like T. B.

*Liana Daskalova*

I prefer Slavic antiquity.
The cat foretelling visitors
by washing itself on the step.
And I, with usual generosity
       lay the table — three rows,
dark wine, a head of white foam
       like dove's down,
and to hear their words - forget
       worries - burning embers.
       A hundred knives quiver, held firm
       in the wood near the bread.
A hundred heroes all ready to leap to my defence:
       that's how it should be.

*Liana Daskalova*

## So Far I Have Kept Dumb

It's time for summer supper,
early outdoors, under newborn stars.
And a bell for evening prayer,
swings between green mountain spurs,
no one crosses themselves, no one trusts it,
each one checks their watch by it
and the sound diminishes so fast
that it trembles like a breath on the sky's glass.
Summer...,
Like a young fleece fields are curly,
smelling of the young, of green,
of something short-lived,transitory.
A firefly flashes in the blue – to vanish,
mayflies are born and die,
everything is like glass – shatters
when you open cupped hands – dust, crushed shell.

As if expecting loss, at evening –
I feel intense pain. For the last time. Before dying
and an immense night under a golden eyebrow
thunders closer and closer
                as it presses me low.
Summer meadows are fragrant – but where! Unattainable!
Today will never be repeatable.
Ancient despair devours me in the evening
with a foreboding of darkness and of parting.
So far I have kept dumb, but now I ask: – You,
my mortal brethren, do you feel such despair
draining you,
     in the evening
                voyagers of the unvoyageable?
Well then, I devour you. Devotedly. Before death.

Liana Daskalova

## This Life

I never wanted boredom in this life,
just strife,
a feast was what I wanted out of life!

I've worn the dawn round my neck, pure and white—
a hundred and one pearls in one long necklace,
a trinket, and ear-rings
like tiny grapes,
clasped fingers within cupped hands —
like cherries in a child's basket,
on my feet — evening shoes, soaring
on gusts and waetzes, equally defenceless...

But who would have dreamed of protection, rules or the need to
                                                            defend
of dancing on thorns, of blood or of wound upon wound?

I wanted to make a feast of life, my life,
to dance through it — but my youth, inexperience...

But when the guardian cypresses rose up in anger,
and peacocks in the night shrilled — haughtily, ominously,
and when rings tumbled from my pale finger,
and when the air alighted on my shoulder
and started to peck my neck with two beaks of eagles,
and earth and stone burst in flames beneath my heels,
and there melted the little fingers of children,

*Liana Daskalova*

and neither water, nor wine — nothing and no one
to extinguish them,
        no trace of any help
and I was running, sparks coming from shoes ablaze
like fireflies,
when I ran like a beggar, catching for breath,
ablaze I ran — and created my new cruel
manner of writing
        for that fiery breath...

# Lilyana Stefanova
# (1929 – )

Lilyana Stefanova was born in Sofia. She studied at the Moscow Institute of Literature and between 1965 and 1967 was a postgraduate student in London. In 1980 Lilyana Stefanova was involved in the writers' programme of the University of Iowa in the USA. She has attended writers' forums in Tokyo, New York, London, Paris and Brussels.

Lilyana Stefanova has over 30 volumes of poetry, prose, and essays to her credit. Her works contain recurrent themes and images in which feminine emotions reside alongside the problems and rhythm of the world. Her verses are tense and sometimes dramatic and challenging.

Lilyana Stefanova is a prominent public figure in Bulgaria and has been the long-standing President of the Bulgtarian Pen Club and Deputy Minister of Education.

*Lilyana Stefanova*

*Lilyana Stefanova*

## Talent

*Talent — the only novelty
to remain new.*
        Boris Pasternak

In this world
what doesn't grow old?
A spaceship?
The woman you love?
A heart, possessed by the fight for fame?
Unexpected news
like a crash of thunder?

And hymns
sung with a clear heart,
and feelings,
raging within us,
and earthly desires
like beads
scattered when time was forgotten.

Yesterday's sensation —
is nothing new today.
A town square
crossed by flip-flops.
Words rolled
in summer-show bedding.
And sufficiency
instead of divine hunger.

*Lilyana Stefanova*

And tricks —
long since performed;
at God knows what meridian,
on one short wave or another...
Don't you know? It's a new state!
Which one?
Kiribati.
In the midst of the Pacific...
That's nothing new!

And strangely enough —
in this world
that has perhaps reached its ceiling
and is tired to death of sensation —
it is the talent that stays forever new.
Rediscovered.
Reborn.

*Lilyana Stefanova*

# When I Feel Sad

When I feel unhappy—
my clothes are bright.
In the dance of colour,
in the frivolity
of carefree patterns
the sorrow
remains concealed,
dignified and proud,
without appeal.

Everyone says:
how colourful and well you look.
So what happened
this autumn day?
Bright colours
net the sorrow
so it can't touch me.

Colours
with merry voices become
a barrier,
a protection,
a life-saving sea-wall.

However bad I feel —
I always find
shelter in their brilliance
a shelter unseen by
another's eye.

*Lilyana Stefanova*

They play a wise game.
They guard me from
giving up when life's at its worst,
with will broken.
Any attempt by this sorrow
to shout out
is in vain.
colours speak louder.

A whirlwind of colour —
to prevent the search for comfort,
to hold you upright
in your own
independent world!
If you meet me some day
wearing bright clothes —
believe in them —
those colours!

*Lilyana Stefanova*

\* \* \*

Nothing could be scarier.
Nothing.
The man you love,
calling out another name in his sleep.
And in the night, in that moonless castle,
another name echoes
like a threat,
like a funeral bell.

You're in bed.
You hear the pulse of the empty house.
Dawn knits feeble strands.
He wakes.
Embraces you.
Innocent and pure as a child.

*Lilyana Stefanova*

* * *

Our souls are together.
Why?
Long time ago
like a cobweb
everything between us
was torn down —
we made
no effort to preserve any of it.
Not even the most important part.
What was it?
We've forgotten.
How many days is it since your coat
huddled on the peg next to mine.
Long ago.

But our reckless souls
are still together
bound by pristine tenderness.
Why?

*Lilyana Stefanova*

# The Bracelet

The whole night
I've been trying
to slip the moon
onto my wrist
like a bracelet.
But I couldn't.
Is this why I feel
such pain in my wrist
and this fire
in my soul?

Before it was so easy.
I walked —
they stopped
to stare in amazement:
daring
to make the moon a bracelet —
she must be crazy!

The unattainable
was so simple —
I just reached for it.
Any magic
was always first -
and never
last.

If I sense
that I'm losing
the magic anguish after the miracle,
how could I go on living?
so I never stop.
Each attempt hurts me.
But I know I can't live
without it.

*Lilyana Stefanova*

## An Empty Sky

Never before
has this shore
been so deserted.
Gulls,
sails,
salt-sea winds,
mussel shells,
sunrises —
all fled.
Or else my soul
can no longer see anything!
What made them
abandon me
to follow you?
How
A curse?
Or magic?
Why didn't you leave
at least one
distant sail on the horizon?

As far as the eye can see
a deserted shore.
And an empty sky
under which
I have nowhere to hide.

Lilyana Stefanova

## A Blue Streak in the Sky

Until yesterday — it was clear,
but today a mist has crept in.
I can't understand —
why I didn't slam the door on it.
But how could I ?
The mist — cold
and clammy
within me.
I tried everything.
I can't hope for anything more.
Coldness —
settled unceremoniously
in my soul.

Why do we
sometimes look like an airport
with all flights cancelled?
To all destinations:
the flight to faith,
the flight to hope,
the flight to simple joys.

Cancelled — until further notice.
It's so depressing
to have wings
when there's no visibility
in your soul.
And yet clear-eyed skies.

*Lilyana Stefanova*

Will there ever be a wind
to chase away this mist,
this inner darkness?
All flights are cancelled.
But high
above the mountain tops —
a blue streak in the sky,
as in a child's notebook.

And a sign within my soul.

# Stanka Pencheva
# (1929 – )

Stanka Pencheva was born in Sliven. She studied Russian language and literature at Sofia Universisty and has published more than 10 volumes of poetry and essays. Stanka Pencheva is a distinctive voice on the literary scene and is especially popular among women. Her poems are deeply imaginative and thoughtful, appealing to the ordinary person and contemporary woman, who try to maintain their balance and spirituality in an unbalanced and unsophisticated world. Her poetry is outstandingly open and authentic, full of femininity and love of life.

*Stanka Pencheva*

*Stanka Pencheva*

## Advice to Myself

Don't compare your self to your fellow men.
Don't look for comfort in those weaker than yourself.
Don't feast your eyes
on your peacock feathers.

Be wicked and discontented!
Like Jacob wrestle with the gods,
be envious of Sappho,
compare yourself to geniuses –
so that
impotence will bring you to tears.
Write frantically,
write in horrendous pain,
write like one on death row,
or like a sibyl,
write in such a way
that blood will drip from your fingertips,
in such a way
that the paper chars...

Stanka Pencheva

# Planets

They've been lying side by side —
probably since the creation of the world —
woman and man.
He sleeps arms outstretched,
a heavy, rugged trunk,
hewn down by the axe of sleep.
Across his face
now rabies, now triumph —
he sleeps, in chain-mail,
like a warrior,
combat still in the blood,
in fists,
in the hoarse cry...

Flooding from the darkness
is a nacreous, dim light:
rounded with ebbs and flows,
with warm knees bent,
the woman sleeps.
In a meadow.
On a cloud.
On a man's arm.
Sleep
soaks into the quiet body
like rain.
The woman sleeps -
given up and trusting.
... Circling in cosmic darkness,
lonely and distant, two planets.
The Saturn ring shines softly
upon the arms
of the woman and the man.

*Stanka Pencheva*

# A Monologue by Eve

This is Paradise — an orchard.
I am the beautiful gardener.
The man sleeps in the shade of the fig-tree —
he doesn't yet know about my gift.
If he had his way, until the end of time
he would wallow in this heavenly sphere,
weighed down by over-eating, a flower behind his ear,
chaste and foolish. If I wasn't here...
But I am.
And in a little while I shall shake
that bough with the single apple.
I shall pretend to long for a bite of it,
say it's the sweetest thing in Paradise.
The man, called Adam, will at last notice
that the fruit on my tree is also ripe...
How long will it take to teach him to be tender!
How long — to risk, to learn courage!
He would crawl in dust before God's wrath
(banished means free!)
Out of fear he'll create fire
out of hunger he'll hunt in the woods.
I'll bear children, polish his weapons,
I'll smile mysteriously, unheard...
But now, when I pick the apple,
I already know —
there'll also be Newton...

Stanka Pencheva

# The Great Game

The rules of this game, dearest, are as follows:
you go first.
I am mysterious and silent.
You spread out all your feathers,
you break the antlers of all your rivals.
I am tempting and unfaithful.
Then you frown like a threatening cloud,
you smoke too much, and walk alone until late,
your passion becomes white-hot –
when at last I show mercy.
What follows is a stellar whirlwind, a deluge, radiation,
there are no dates, laws, road signs,
our boat forever rides foaming crests,
you are in me, and I in you...
And here, my darling, the game ends imperceptibly –
because we are punished by a long and arduous love.
Because the forest around us is raw and damp
we must break from ourselves –
    so as to feed the fire.
Time patiently whets its knife –
we cannot escape...
Screeching birds
come to scratch in the garden of our soul.
And collecting its train is the star of wonder, the tailed one.

From now on, darling, we'll go on foot. No more flying.
And if you get too tired –
just lean on me.

*Stanka Pencheva*

# Declaration of Love

I love you with all my body —
you give back to it the pure sound
and the folly,
otherwise called youth.

I love you with all my mind —
you drop poison into my thoughts,
you stir up passion to be your equal,
the anguish — to surpass myself...

I love you with all the maternity in me —
my eyes are open
to your sweet vanity,
to your fits of cowardice,
to your tiredness,
to your fear of pain
and death...
It's then I tenderly embrace you.

I love you with all my imagination —
you share
all my festive games,
the childish fairs,
our pilgrimages
amid streams and trees.
With you I become a sorceress,
a stargazer,
a poet...

I love you with all my sadness.
With the uncomfortable coolness of growing old.
With the women's dread of loneliness.
With the bitterest of feelings —
about the limit of talent.

*Stanka Pencheva*

I love you with my dress
which touches you,
and with words I grope for,
I love you with the entire world —
because you are in it,
I love you with my little finger,
I love you out of habit —
and like the budding of a miracle,
I love you to humiliation,
I love you triumphantly!...

How else can I explain it to you?
— It's as if I'm writing
on water...

Stanka Pencheva

# Belated Experiment

*The alchemist says: "My son, take two ounces
of mercury and three ounces of spite..."*
Book of Alchemy. V. L. Rabinovich

I mixed in, still water, herbs and tender anguish,
apple blossom, sweet self-delusions,
a cricket's leg, a firefly's wing...and that's all.
I kept it on the boil over a moderate fire.
The potion proved useful – for spleen and for pangs of love.
...But why did I never try to throw into molten lead
three ounces of spite, blood of a neighbour,
tooth of a snake, fear and meanness, the hair of a despot,
a lonely cry...
And fire, fire! Let the flames lick
the seething flask with fervent passion and anger!

But its too late to start again. My fire flickers faintly.
Somewhere something else seethes
angrily, cruelly.

Stanka Pencheva

## The Circus Is Leaving

It's all over, the circus is leaving:
tent — folded away, the tigers — in the cage,
only the wind still whistles,
only — holes where poles once stood, and footprints,
only — a bright circle of saw-dust...
Save a crushed ticket from the grass
so that when you walk in the rain of years,
that luminous cupola will soar above your head,
and the roll of drums stir your spirit.
And through all that face-slapping, those cups of vinegar,
may laughter forever remain
painted on your face.

*Stanka Pencheva*

# Something Like an Auto-Epitaph

It seems to me that all my life I've been sewing
with the same needle.
Only the thread's changed, now black, now white
and now glasses perched upon my nose.
Once I sewed a button while the shirt was still worn –
and my blood felt the sweet blood of man;
I sewed my mother's shroud and the winter
penetrated as deep as my heart; I've sewed in sorrow
and in jubilation; I've stitched carefully what was torn
by thorns, rough handling, or unloving.
I sewed silk and air. And ugly wounds.
I sewed rancour. And sometimes – benediction.
A woman like me, who travels often,
still carries her eternal needle in her luggage.
I hope that in the beyond, it will still come in useful:
to patch up black holes and angels' wings...

Stanka Pencheva

## The Season of Losses

I'm out of sorts. I don't know why.
I'm neither alone, nor sick,
a bright flower blossoms in my room,
I work, I make do with very little.
Where then did this sharp pebble come from?
Actually – I know:
I can't stand the season.
I work as before, but
I don't step into the risk zone
of magnetic anomalies,
of frenzies, of vertigoes.
My love has abated, it has kindled
a soft fire, it's cutting bread for two.
But the old story will never be repeated –
it has drained the well in my heart...
Am I any wiser? – A little more experience on the outside,
superiority – on the face,
but inside – the same girl:
still clapping her hands, now slightly aged,
getting out of breath, yet trying hard to run,
closing eyes to all that's frightening...

I am out of sorts No comfort. Dark and dank.
I'll get used to it, no choice – my season
descends the slope of losses.
All I can do is face it with dignity.

# Nadya Kehlibareva
# (1933–1988)

Nadya Kehlibareva was born in Sofia and brought up in the Black Sea port of Varna. The sea has greatly influenced her poetry, not just as a poetic theme, but as a constant companion of her freedom-loving spirit. The three most frequently used words in her poetry are "multi-coloured", "beauty" and "smile". They are the substance of her poems; joy at the miracle of life and impulsive faith in huamn goodness.

Nadya Kehlibareva also wrote poetry for children and has published books of sketches dedicated to ordinary working people. Nadya Kehlibareva studied French language and literature and translated into Bulgarian from French and German.

Her last volume of verse *Edin Zhivot ne Stiga* (One Life Is Not Enough) was published in 1988 after her death. It sounds a deeply tragic note. Her last brief poems are a cry for human warmth before the long, long coldness.

*Nadya Kehlibareva*

*Nadya Kehlibareva*

# Heiress

I was brought up by the last strip of land.
But the land beyond those dunes is also mine.
It so happens — I don't sleep at night
but listen to the talk
        of tide and sand, wood and shade,

and how my past calls out across the centuries,
and my future responds to it —
        heavy with celestial grapes...
Then day breaks. And in the garden a drop of dew
already shines - the tear of a rose.

Nadya Kehlibareva

# A Page from an Old Book

You sea-farer, knock it into your sons' heads
to feed courage
             with reason, and stay humble.
Keep repeating it loudly so they'll remember
their heavy catch is the sea.

Although faltering, over-worked,
although sweating blood with fatigue –
let them always have dominion over it.
And it will keep moving, with its emerald bosom,
through the net of ages –
uncaught, always uncaught....

*Nadya Kehlibareva*

# Breaking Point

Why does the tear shine
when so many of our wounds
      stay hidden?
Why does the earth slip from under our feet
when we are threatened by despair?

At such an hour we never know
      if oat fields sway in the wind
or if snow will come with its heavy cloak...
At such an hour we hang ourselves.
Or we start,
      seemingly pathetic, from scratch.

*Nadya Kehlibareva*

# A Bright Patch

Not to invent, Lord,
but to write plainly
about the need for sunlight. About tiredness.
About people's
        joy and pain.

To know that my fast road is descending.
No needless worries to weigh down on me.
In silence
     to look for lyrics,
until cooped up in my earthen home.

*Nadya Kehlibareva*

# Omen

In the evening, I spy mother. At a bridge, a staircase.
Coming to me,
        when I get back from work.
A heavy key hanging from her thigh,
she says: — I left a black well
        open to the stars.

She says; —Let's go down together.
Because of loneliness
        I'll soon forget how to speak...
A slice of moon swims after us.
And a traffic light with its red eye
        frightens, trips up swarms of people.

I feel so good with mother. Happy, at ease.
A bright caress floats in the night air.
Snow powders us in early autumn.
I've lost my summer shoes
        and splash barefoot in puddles.

I feel so good with mother. Sweet and sad.
She says: — Hush! The final pain
        sends its omen to all...
My dear, dead mother, should I lie to you
saying I'm ready and have no fear?

*Nadya Kehlibareva*

## Things not Said

You will forget my voice. And my laughter.
Was it only me who laughed
        now merrily, now with bitterness?
You will forget whether I was or was not,
crumbly as white sandstone.

You will forget my quiet hands. Even
my honey-sweet words
        asking for caress, for pardon.
You will forget that I made a God-like sun shine
for you even at night.

You will forget which of us was caring,
and who – never cared
        on our short holidays.
But you'll remember, you'll remember for ever
how I sobbed in my sleep...

# Ekaterina Yossifova
## (1941 – )

Ekaterina Yossifova was born in the town of Kyustendil. She is one of the few poets not living in Sofia. She studied language and worked as a teacher, theatre director and editor. Her first volume of poetry appeared in 1959 and more followed. Ekaterina Yossifova's poems are rooted in Bulgarian folk songs but also have wider European and universal human appeal. She is a sensistive modern poet and her refined intellect is ever present. Ekaterina Yossifova's means of expression are laconic, yet each combination of words carries many meanings, resulting in simplicity and lightness. Her poetry has the appeal of a well-cut crystal.

*Ekaterina Yossifovu*

*Ekaterina Yossifova*

# If Only I Hadn't Been so Distracted

If only I hadn't been so distracted,
I would have grown old by now.
I fancy that age: a house to comfort you,
a tree to support you,
everything supporting you.

If I think hard I'll remember what I've lost.
Well, I've not actually lost it, it lost itself.
It wasn't me who abandoned it, my life did.
Only I must never forget what I first
considered important.

Others enter, usually
out of love.
Besides, at every turn, something
is waiting, it's in the air, and there's only one hazard:
to be a child, unhappy in a room full of toys.

It's the same as before: you stand on one shore
and gaze across at the other.
And the fast current makes you dizzy.
What was important then?
If I think hard I may remember.

Ekaterina Yossifova

Only the water shifts, dry beds
hollowed out long ago by floods of love.
Must I traverse them
in order to see where they lead?
Grass grows, thistles grow, a cosmic bug walks.

I could have been a long way off by now
in a direction no longer mine.
And this day, sluggishly flowing between my eye-lashes,
could have been so desperately short.
If only I hadn't been so distracted.

*Ekaterina Yossifova*

\* \* \*

You said: I want us to do something together,
even if it's just to make a den of twigs.

You sa id: I'd rather leave man naked
from time to time, alone with fire.

You said: Nothing is more beautiful than reason,
and the reason of all reasons is sentiment.

You said: Don't be afraid.
We didn't give in to youth,
let alone old age!

*Ekaterina Yossifova*

# Granny

She is a loving soul,
small and white.
Her home's small too,
you can go on foot.

She enjoys it all,
accepts it as good:

my uncle's address
from a far off land,
my grandad's whiskers
above a starched band
(He's young, and waits
to walk her, hand in hand).

Quickly, early, lovingly
she orders her garden:
welcoming each blade,
as each sod gives birth.

By the way, she's long since
gone under the acacia tree.
And whatever they may say,
her secret dream's with me:

A warm breath floats by,
quivering leaf, quivering sound —
outside life whistles
through her bird-like bones.

Ekaterina Yossifova

## The Mirror

*To Leda Tasseva**

Here's a face. What exactly does it reveal?
It's my face, my face in a mirror.
A bit rumpled
by so many attractions.

A face like any other face: sins have piled up
yet some innocence is left.
Nothing special, but sometimes a thirst
to run against the wind of justice.

A face like any other face. Transience has made it nervous,
so it constantly blocks the view with its hair,
There was a time when it seemed
to wear a secret on its lips.

And how did it all end: nothing
turned out to be real. Faces in a mirror.
Like beings who act
for beings who act out their lives.

* Leda Tasseva was a Bulgarian actress

*Ekaterina Yossifova*

## Work

While I'm waiting
let's do something useful.

It's a temporary refuge,
and I'm only a guest.

Everyone can understand:
you make something to last, a house, a chair, a child.

Something against nonsense
to whom it makes no difference.

Much was ruined
but the making remained.

It won't bring you to your feet,
yet you'll still find it props you up.

What hasn't passed through work's hands?
Lately, it's getting older,
Only the other day it was sat on a bench,
and still there when I came back from the shop.
And the garden went without water.

*Ekaterina Yossifova*

\* \* \*

I suspect
words of cunning.
           And silence – of facelessness.
Tension clawing within our smiles,
           our tears dry.
I suspect the criminal of good intentions.
The ruler – of impotence.
The wise man – of folly. I suspect the past: an ikebana
           of dried flowers, curved twigs.
I suspect the artist of forcing the picture
           into the frame of his own desires.
I suspect the friend of being alien
           and the stranger – an old acquaintance.
I suspect unhealed wounds,
           and those that heal too fast.
I suspect the heavenly bank
           of bankruptcy.
I suspect myself: of making my life
           merely a poor copy of life.

*Ekaterina Yossifova*

## Sirius

I can't see much
from where I'm standing:
a small depression between two folds of earth.

I guess about most things,
but what I like best
is to open myself up to naive light.

It's then I feel secure
as if someone has confirmed
all my secret hopes with a nod.

Perhaps, star, it's you.
Why ask, when I see you shine,
that should be enough.

*Ekaterina Yossifova*

\* \* \*

It's your fair I'm going to.

I'm taking my old fur, my five-year-old mac,
and the fields will be swarthy, and the sky — bright blue.
On the way I know so well, legs are in a merry mood
and if I start on time, I'll see a thin pink haze.

I'll step on the path
worth nothing, yet gold can't buy it.
I'll meet the root of loyalty
and the blossom of untalkative lips.

I'll stay quiet concealing my hundred tongues,
and only eavesdrop: from a nightingale's crop,
from these muddy hills, like ugly bellies
of delivered women where future grapes gently swing.

Your hand is infinite,
again you put days aside for me.

Your hand is infinite for me and others
violets smell indifferently
small rumours leap lightly
on small islands of wintered-tufts
a light drizzle for any who pass by
consolation and a tiny tear for no apparent reason.

Your hand is infinite and perhaps at the last moment
I'll manage to stay beneath it.
Twinkling like a star
tiny as a poppy seed
deluded like me and deluding itself.
Support me again today for my daily bread
for my daily hunger and daily shame.

Ekaterina Yossifova

# Earth

Tucked away somewhere inside there
the deceived body will learn by itself
how to thaw, slides down without hurry, without hunger
towards its quiet billionth hell,
it's no consolation, nor is it sinister:
there's too little space for immobility.

# Rada Alexandrova
# (1943 – )

Rada Alexandrova was born in Svilengrad in southern Bulgaria. She has published seven volumes of poetry and two plays. Her poetry breathes earth, fire and intensive life, greatly influenced by the region of her birth. She has been living and working in Sofia for a long time, yet she is not a city poet. Her whole being and hence her verses are imbued with vitality. People in her poetry do not "go back" to nature but are an intrinsic part of it. She writes about "that world for which I became a home". There is a kind of "magic realism" about her poetry which is purely Bulgarian and strongly linked to folklore and popular legends, to herbs and magic spells. Rada Alexandrova's poetry conveys a sense of transience and eternity, her world dramatically destroys itself only to be rebuilt. Her works are full of complex analogies which are open to different interpretations.

*Rada Alexandrova*

*Rada Alexandrova*

# Summer

And summer descended
along its river.
A green whirlwind of a summer
falling like
the high wild waves
of years now over.
Summer was once
a song of green.

I felt its dark rumble
like an inborn longing –
you can never bring it back,
nor can you stop it.
It nibbled the frothy, crumbly
fine shores.
It nibbled worms and snails
and they nibbled it.

It was huge and swelling –
unending, undying,
like a dragon from a fearsome tale,
a dreamed-up sea,
like a ripe deserted field,
like a single poppy.
It gathers us up into a yellow flower.
And then sheds us again.

Rada Alexandrova

It's long since we stood in its cusp,
nor do we walk
along the path taken years ago by the greedy,
swooping river.
Even if we were stars and stones,
a legend or a moving mass –
you wouldn't like it
you wouldn't stop it.

Rada Alexandrova

# Voices

*To Gergana*


I heard the voices of happy women —
darkness brought them.
And the taut string of the leaning moon
resounding.

I heard the wind gathering seeds,
and walnuts cracking.
Within me sounds piled up
as in a fathomless chasm.

And I heard the great winds
groaning, shrieking, hammering.
And I drank silently
from those earthy yet unearthly voices.

The sparkling voice of the yellow bee,
the red voice of the stone,
and the dark voice of blue mountain ridges
flared up triumphantly.

Stalactites, ice, hope
and despair rumbled.
And how soft the voices
of the blonde clouds.

Now I am the echo of distant worlds,
of fern, of aftermath...
I don't even know which of my voices
to leave behind for you.

Rada Alexandrova

# At Night

*In memory of Andrei Ghermanov*

It's quiet, quiet, so quiet
in the round home of night.
Perhaps it's you who called me
to light your candle.

Perhaps I was lit
simply to melt away.
Four drops of coral,
earth, and eyes beneath the earth.

And in the windless silence,
in the slow lamp of night,
my short wick is lit
and gently pierces the earth.

Perhaps – it's to finish reading
your invisible life,
while my sharp eye
outlines the contours.

Perhaps – it's so I can still
keep you, and forever,
be the simple rhyme
that's also in the purest layer.

To read your faces
with all those secrets,
perhaps it was me they sent
to light the candle.

*Rada Alexandrova*

\* \* \*

*To Elissaveta Bagryana*


In the garden three yellow stalks grow.
And my beloved is as handsome as sorrow.

Battles hang over children and boughs.
Yet he was never banished from my soul.

Drought hit us, and the house left in havoc.
And my dear one is like a long cool gulp.

The sea level rose by ten spans.
And he looks at me with golden eyes.

Last night moon poured into a hollow bone.
How well I hear him in the distance stepping out alone.

How long has it rained — a day, an eternity,
yet I'm alive — a drop in his body.

I live — alive in the earth's womb,
it saps me, to the waist in the tomb,

I moved away the stone, my loved one sat near me.
In his hand — my hand, parting company.

Rada Alexandrova

## Where

When I dwindle to nothing,
what will happen to those mountains
which grew up in me.
To the greenish swamps
with bubbles in them
and to the voices of midnight reeds.
To the moon
which emerged so furiously
from the well of my heart.
And to time,
which runs out only to return
like a worn out horseman,
made from bronze.
Can they be burned straw,
those eyes of my beloved
and that journey
which continues
in my essence.
(I hear his steps
in my pulse
and in the anguish of the black headscarf
hoeing the vineyard once again).
What river will
that sea pour away into,
that rock in my breast,
and the fish,
and the sunlit islands.
The stars, and the fog,
and the universe,
and this world,
whose home I became,
where will they move to?

*Rada Alexandrova*

\* \* \*

Have mercy on us, mercy on the merciless days,
mercy on the Jenny Wren, and on the ginger maple,
mercy on the dry lips of the dying,
and on the unknown blind man, born out of mercy.

Mercy on this crumpled bedding,
and on the eyes which haul you outwards,
and on the cricket, the germ, mercy on that step
from the radiant world to the last sleep.

O Lord, never seen, you remote mother,
mercy on this small pulsating land,
like a tiny helpless fist in someone's eternity,
whose postnatal bowels still smoulder.

Mercy, good fellow, I beg you have mercy, on her —
blood-stained by vanity, with scooped up flesh,
mercy on the air that lives in cruelty,
and on the doomed dying waters.

I will peep in to your soul, severe and approaching,
and will pour out through the waves of pain.
I will send you a twig and blossom
with maternal farewell mercy from a luck-giving hand.

Rada Alexandrova

\* \* \*

*And he went a little farther, and fell on his face, and prayed,
saying, O my Father, if it be possible, let this cup pass from me.*
Matthew xxxvi. 39

This cup did not pass from us, did not pass from us.
And a boundless, unknown winter covered the land.
And we fell on our faces like criminals,
and we heard the screaming of our hearts, we heard the thunder.

And then we arose stiff and numb, to walk again,
and we were the known and the unknown, and we were many...
And neither the sun, nor Golgotha lay before us,
and we walked onwards like the dead beyond all life.

And the raging wilderness hurled fire into the eyes,
and like others he fell upon his face by the wayside.
And only the wind turned back to bewail him
and snow filled his mouth with sky and storm.

And again it came about that it whirled up in frenzy,
and it came to pass we gnawed stars like jackals,
and over the chest streamed blood, clods of earth, lumps of ice.
And neither were we the first nor the last.

And was it not that we soared through blue infinity towards
                                                    Paradise
without memory, without feet, mother, breath, or name?
What were we, whose were we? From what motherland came we
                                                    hence?
This cup did not pass from us, did not pass from us...

*Rada Alexandrova*

* * *

From out of memory, from the ashes
summer fluttered innocently.
And this hot-peaked autumn
walks towards other summers.

A thin, sweet smoke gushed out
to cover the small town,
my lost Sundays,
and the breast of coming winters.

And the short-lived idle breeze
shook down at full moon
gold coins from remote July –
leaves – the eyes of a saint.

I came so slowly into this world,
and yet how fast it leaves!
A stack of sparkling chaff flares up,
lit amidst fallow fields.

And in this autumn-pervaded home,
whatever I have collected
clearly passes me by.
And left a little earlier.

# Kalina Kovacheva
(1943 – )

Kalina Kovacheva was born in the village of Bozhourlouka in northern Bulgaria and was brought up in the Danubian town of Svishtov. She studied Bulgarian language and literature at Veliko Turnovo University and has published four volumes of poetry, two short novels and several filmscripts.

Kalina Kovacheva's poetic presence is restrained and self-possessed but very interesting. She never allows feelings to transform into feminine sentimentality, reflections into dull philosophisng or originality into eccentricity. Discriminating and sparing in her means of expression, Kovacheva is relentlessly ironic towards herself. She is sarcastic and yet overflowing with coy tenderness and tragic awareness.

Critics often speak of a "poetic voice". In modern Bulgarian poetry Kalina Kovacheva's voice is distinctly heard because of her natural intonations and the unexpected and unaffected way she begins her poems, as if in mid-sentence, thus arriving at her truths.

*Kalina Kovacheva*

Kalina Kovacheva

\* \* \*


They say: He's far away.
I say: We breathe the same air.
They say: He's forgotten you.
I say: Words keep their meaning.
They say: Perhaps he's kissing another?
I say: It's my lips he wants to remember.
They say: You're always alone. Wrapped in thought.
I say: I want to remember his lips.
They say: Your poems have become sadder.
I say: Sadness is the shadow of happiness.
They say: You've become a shadow yourself.
I say: The body will always fly after the soul.
They say: But life is shorter now...
I say: At least Death is eternal.
They say: You're odd. Such love is not reality.
I say: You are poor. But there's a knock at the door.
They say: Perhaps its the wind again.
        I have no lips to answer.

Kalina Kovacheva

\* \* \*

While I'm away wasting ripe moments
one by one — red cranberries in the woods
and spruce needles on the moss, bald for lack of warmth,
while I'm away searching for ripe moments
to tell me who I am, what I am, and why,
while I'm away:
a friend will pass my door, forgetting he could enter
to tell me of his pain, and hear of mine
over a glass of wine, to agree in the end that the world is great,
even when it hurts and you are slowly dying;
the child will forget my laughter, will forget I only laughed
at its laughter — fragile and sincere,
and may it always be sincere and may only
the laughter be fragile, that one thing that made me
laugh;
my beloved will knock, but when he senses
that the void remains speechless, unlit by any genuine gesture
and when his gesture finds no response,
it will perhaps lift the burden from his heart, because
my love is a daily risk, and risk
for man is a military command, not a joy;
and my enemy, only my enemy will remember
and wait for me to come,
grown old and empty,
having found nothing but red cranberries in the woods
and spruce needles on the moss, bald through lack of warmth.
While I'm away...

*Kalina Kovacheva*

\* \* \*


He said: You talk to gods —
so how can I ask you to wash my socks!
He went away, obsessed with fear
and married an untalented woman.
I'm left at the end of the earth.
There I am, dangling legs over its edge,
perhaps not even knowing who I am
(or may be I'm my own memorial).
Words run along my veins
to gather in the frail vessel
of my heart.
        And they hurt, hurt, hurt,
until they flash in me intermittently.
Upon the taut wire of nerves
and in my seismic brain — at night
my poem is born — unmarked by luck
but crumpled, bloody and dishevelled.
And I record these fearful lines,
but there's no one to send them to.
Yes, perhaps I do talk to the gods.

But I dream of washing socks.

Kalina Kovacheva

\* \* \*

And words never obey me,
they only nod gently and leave
transparent, spooky and hospitably chill —
just like childhood with bruised heels
along a sluggish green-eyed stream
with the glint of silvery fish-scales;
just like my father when he left
that the day of high hopes;
just like the dark-skinned man,
who politely inclined his head when I invited him
to drop in just for a few moments,
just to throw on a glowing ember yet the fireplace
burst into flames;
like the child who pretends to listen,
but who already knows more
than I;
like life which I appear to put to rights,
yet the thread seems frayed and shortened
and one day, darkness will suddenly fall —
and so words never obey me,
but slightly nod and leave
dropping in the nest down the road
waiting for someone greater than I
to pass by and wake them
in a day,
in a hour,
in a few centuries.

Kalina Kovacheva

\* \* \*

Disasters enveloped me — schools of fish
bodies voluptuous, lustrous, summer flesh,
schools of lightnings, comets,
of fears. And unrhymed verse.
Disasters knocked on my door — or hit me
head on, suddenly, guiltily
with the eyes of a lizard or a friend.
(I've also seen disaster in the image of a cow).
Many disasters dropped in —
one was even my recent guest
and remained there — by the window,
a beloved disaster, but still a disaster.
                      Well, disasters may simply
be in love with me. Most probably
they're courting. And are jealous.
Somehow advancing with disastrous lust
towards my obstinate smile.
They bring me flowers. So clever
to hide their poisonous odour.
I put them in a vase
and smile once again — summer ice.
So if you ever meet up with a disaster —
pale, frozen, huddled and lost,
I'll be there looking out for it — so just
give my latest address.
— Feel free — I'll say — it goes without saying
I'm delighted to see you,
And if the disaster proves bigger than my house,
I'll make the chimney into a chair.

Kalina Kovacheva

* * *

The woman with the string-bag is my mother. She carries the bread.
In her other hand — the change, the key and the milk.
She goes up the stairs, when my cry grips her:
— Wait!
She goes up the stairs, and her outdated movements are now so
slow.
(Wasn't it only yesterday she was womanly-girlish?)
She goes up slowly. And the cry reaches her:
— Love us!
If I could only stop her at the foot of the stairs. With the milk.
With the bread in the bag, with her eyes. With her eyes!
If only I could have stopped her before the long climb—
that upward flight.
what will I actually say? Mother, dear mother, be careful,
if only I could lead you back to the foot of the stairs,
if we could lie at your feet for a while
like doves.
If we could stay. All of us together. Down there.
At the lowest point of those stairs you have to climb.
With your eyes, your hair, your despair:
— Wait!

But you go up. Up the stairs. Up.
And you carry the bread.

*Kalina Kovacheva*

\* \* \*

It was Someone – midnight. Cigarette smoke,
a breath of wine, words, still trickling.
Neither friend, nor brother, but a total stranger,
evil and clever.
It was Someone. I said nothing. Grew tame with fear,
mewing like a cat, pitifully.
He seemed to tremble with cold, but told me calmly
he was hungry.
But what could I offer? Look at the table – only
a piece of bread and an exhausted soul.
The bread was hard. But he seized and worried it.
He ignored the soul.
A gulp of wine? No? Anyway there didn't seem
to be any left in my bottle.
Yet he tipped it and drank. It almost satisfied him.
He asked for a cloak.
I also gave him a shawl – the snow thick outside
as in a poem from ancient times,
he took the gloves. Then dropped the latch.

He ignored the soul.

Kalina Kovacheva

* * *

He makes safe his door with a special lock,
he could keep a dog, but he's good enough on his own –
one day he'll probably start to bark furiously,
if the quiet burglar stops close by.
But what does he lock away with such great care?
A gramophone with worn out needle and no records,
old newspapers, a faded carpet,
and in the carpet – the moths' nest,
a withered geranium in a plastic yoghurt pot,
shirts – two of them almost disabled,
photographs rosy round distant–cheeked
(he was once a child, could you ever believe it?)
But why does he lock away with such great care?
He looks a little like the stooge
who looks intelligent, but stays quiet, because
if he unlocks his mouth,
it will instantly become clear –
that nobody's there.
The lock is to deceive the thieves.

Kalina Kovacheva

\* \* \*

A happy man never writes poetry,
nor does he compose music, or paint pictures.
A happy man never floats into the unknown
remaining unattracted by peaks and ravines
and he is happy with his rulers.
A happy man drinks beer
watches the match,
his wife dumbly slaving away, the two children already in bed.
He too will soon be in bed
without ever dreaming –
a happy man has no dreams.
A happy man is time, stopped
at the height of the feast –
midnight on New Year's Eve.
The old year has passed,
but the new one will never come.
Yet – some lunatic will appear,
a wretch, a mountaineer or a poet,
and he will release the hands of time –
so that it will start to flow again.
And again
the happy man
will be happy.

# Miryana Basheva
# (1947 – )

In the 1970s Miryana Basheva was the recognised spokeswoman of young people. *Tezhuk Harakter* (Difficult Character), the first of her two books was published in 1976 and was a strong and categorical debut. Many of her poems have served as lyrics for popular songs.

Miryana Basheva was born in Sofia, and studied English language and literature at Sofia University. She is the poet of the modern city, of alienation, a lonely warrior disappointed with used ideals and hypocritical saints, fighting moral pretension. Those moods, characteristic of young people in Bulgaria (and in the West), are clearly portrayed in Miryana Basheva's verses. Her irony is murderous. She introduces crude, defiantly heedless characters, and uses dialect and slang as well as numerous literary and political allusions. Her aggressive love conceals her spiritual vulnerability.

*Miryana Basheva*

*Miryana Basheva*

\* \* \*

Behind the thorn-crowned forehead
of the genius
(as under the cloth cap
of a lout)
there are instants
of daring
and years
sealed up in a vacuum.
Trifling worries
swinging
on ropes
of steel nerves
"Will it hold?"
Somebody quiet
and grossly incompetent
measures it with a pen-knife.
And the rope
twists,
dangles grimly
like a noose,
and one day
it may just happen
that in all the hurry
someone will tighten it.
Citizens!
Prominent, anonymous,
women-citizens,
countrymen!
Nationals!
Look after each other!
For some of you
may be geniuses.

*Miryana Basheva*

\* \* \*

Scientific yet accessible,
the crystal-clear night shines...
The moon's eyes slyly close,
a bad dream roams the city —
someone's blind fidelity,
homeless barking in a hollow voice.

Needlessly yet inevitably
the sky suspends a medal
above the fiords of streets —
Venus in the fifth house.
Someone's ex-tenderness
snarls through his metal muzzle
with burrs stuck to it.

*Miryana Basheva*

\* \* \*

My foolish, evil star fades
in your blind windows.
Everything is dark. Everything is clear.
You're not there. There's trouble.

Somewhere they may still be breathing.
I'm sure some even bubble with life.
But I don't live. I'm like lichen
taking in oxygen through the skin.

And whenever I see your window lit
by the golden egg of the bedside lamp,
my oxygen-starved heart
turns over like a lizard,
clambers down the curtains,
like night clambering down in summer.
You move your lips, unheard,
bent over coats and suitcases.

*Miryana Basheva*

# The Eighth of December

What appalling behaviour:
tramps like cocks screeching outside,
stretching someone's endless feast
across cobbles at midnight...

And we two are burning low
under the winter-rotten moon:
incredibly good and old...
Amidst chaste silence...
And I, touched by the contrasts
of this funny and frightening city
confide how unhappy I am,
call you true friend and brother...
I sob quietly on your shoulder,
bereaving my intricate schemes...
And you – only you, understand! It's just
that you don't know how to say 'Stop!'

What pleasant variety:
you suffer; you become childishly cruel!
I like this malicious feast
or our daily love-lost!
I like your heavy, snappy,
jealous, helpless hang-over!
I like it when you pay through the nose
for the absence of another.

*Miryana Basheva*

## Business

He comes often. On business.
Honest, hard working... That's all.
But someone is head over heels in love!
And I'm head over heels in pain...

He comes mostly in the evening.
Normally sitting in the corner.
And I feel like game
and my gaze is rounded.

He's not there for personal reasons!...
He leaves pure as an angel...
Clicks the lock monstrously,
as if he's just fettered me.

Like a jailer, he deliberately
strides the stairs.
And I hide from freedom
in a jailhouse of dumbness.

Secretly I sharpen my sword,
my teeth and guillotine blades.
There's more business to be done!
He's bound to return —
after all, what choice does he have...

Miryana Basheva

## You, We and I

*She is our boy.*
V. Samouilov

You
quite sincerely dedicate verses to me
when I'm feeling low.
Shared grief, shared fame,
shared pub bill.

I,
boys, am one of you!
One of you in spirit. And in passing.
Don't all share your bristling.
The muscatel is great today.

You
smile gallantly
at my impudence – to be one of you.
And we write each other – scathing verses.
We defend ourselves. And threaten.

We
are genuine oysters –
opened only by cracking. However...
I
will have to be going.
Say hello to the bar for me.
I
will get a taxi from the square.
I'll manage by myself...
Love to your wives!
And by the way – go jump in the river!

*Miryana Basheva*

# Birthday

Where were you the last twenty-eight,
twenty-eight funny years?
Somewhere near?
In the neighbouring Cosmos?
Under other rainfalls?
Under the same climate?

Another twenty-eight are impending,
twenty eight more mad years.
A life —
ill-cut and carelessly worn out.
High hopes.
Minimum standard of living.

I declare those twenty-eight years a feast,
twenty-eight unpromised years!
But don't leave the table tipsily tipped
across all possible
straight
lines.

Miryana Basheva

## The Wolf Cub

Wolfey, wolf-cub, a wolf's summing-up:
we killed your mother, and you are in a cage.
You don't remember meadows, or hills,
or the bleating of sheep.
And if you did – what would be the use?

And do you remember the frightening stars,
the snow with a blood-stained tracks,
men's boots and the footsteps?

Wolfey, wolf-cub, a wolf's lot,
looking at you – I too could howl!
Sniff me through the iron bars –
I carry the heavy scent
of freedom.

# Vanya Petkova
# (1949 – )

Vanya Petkova was born in Sofia. She studied Slav languages and literature at Sofia University and later studied Spanish in Havana. She has translated Spanish, Arabic, English and German literature into Bulgarian. Vanya Petkova's first poems appeared between 1965 and 1968 and shocked puritans and moralists with the challenging manner in which she reveals female feelings and experiences. The woman in Vanya Petkova's poems refuses to put up with restrictions. Her only law is the law of nature and most of all the law of love as a means of self-expression and absolute freedom. She does not reflect on life and the world. Their harmony and wonder are to be experienced. The sea and the desert, the sultry summer and the sad autumn, love and death coexist side by side in her poetry.

*Vanya Petkova*

*Vanya Petkova*

## Strength

This love is definitely the best,
for it will never happen.
We are swinging on two swings
which constantly pass each other.
The air trembles hot
from your breath like a southern summer
which dries up everything within me,
yet makes me stronger, richer.
I know that I live only through you,
but I sense no fear
that one day you may break the rope
of your swing
and make your way to other worlds
with summer on your breath,
with air between us
and stars crushed beneath our feet.
I have no fear of that death,
for it will never come
to a human so long among flowers,
saturated by their oxygen.
I have no fear of loneliness,
for it will never come
to a human, long swung by love
and untouched by fire.

Vanya Petkova

# Summer

It is barefooted with a torn vest,
with a warm tummy in the bushes,
autumn spills honey and quinces over it
and lights it with lanterns of peaches.
With its small fists it rubs its nose and bursts into tears
for the yellow cat of the Sun,
for unmilked streams, with rose-coloured milk,
for the earth, kneaded into pots.
It's unaware how everyone's waited for it,
how much it has given of itself,
how much eternity it has left behind for a while.
what strong and sensuous signs.
It wanted to grow big,
to grow to the stature of its time,
without being aware that no one
will ever take it to his lap.
It wanted to keep forever
the fruit and the scorching roads,
without ever sensing the quiet
but fatal power of sweetness.
It wanted to have seas
with shores not yet cooled by night,
without ever sensing the great burden
of perseverance.

Barefooted, with a torn vest,
it stands weeping by the dead road,
until with their leaves
trees tuck it away.

*Vanya Petkova*

# By the North Sea

No, I cannot compare to this sea.
Cold kisses shower me
like confetti at a polar festival.
The sea holds out luring lips
and sucks up my steps in a snowy kiss,
while writhing with excitement
for the quick embrace of the woman from the south.
But it's not for me. No, not me. I'm fleeing,
I cannot give myself to you, can't you see,
it would be greater than unfaithfulness,
perhaps even death.
And these pines like steel-clad knights
are descending, descending, like warlike vikings,
and this sand, motionless, soundless,
without the smell of bodies, without forms and falseness,
and this jetty, a dagger stuck in your heart,
and this calmness, ringed with security,
and those emerald-like narrow halls
of your days, uniform and impassive,
choking me.
I cannot give myself to you.
Down there on Europe's thighs
with golden hairs on the dark skin
my sea waits for me with love —
my only love for ever and aye.
There where the sun forgets its thin shuttles
every evening on the shore
and never ending the weaving of its cloth
of moans and a groaning sense of doom.

Vanya Petkova

There where the warmth lies naked
like a mulatto woman with pink nipples
upon the roofs of Sozopol, urging
the hoarse gulls to make love.
There where I'm a woman to the very end,
and the end the beginning of everything,
where paradise is full of sinners
and where it's a sin not to make love.

*Vanya Petkova*

## How Good It Is

How good it is to have wet roofs
and a March sky to roll over them!
How good to have vernal currents
which excruciate and break us into two!
How good that there are men,
like avid roots in the soil
during this season of sweet battles
between flesh and flesh.

How good to be a woman.

But a woman like a bare seashore,
to madly swallow every desire,
like an inevitable flood sweeping over you.
The winds' beaks to grow soft
to peck your small and pointed breasts,
unsatiable waves to creep across you,
and rain's light fingers to grasp you.

How good to be a woman.

To howl like a roe with neck outstretched
amidst bearded bushes and rounded pines,
and to call the males lovingly about you
to snap off their warm antlers.
And to sail without end with new fishermen
to some unfamiliar waters,
and your old age to be blind exhaustion
on the way to a new love.

*Vanya Petkova*

How good to be a woman

at the moment of great fusion,
and with the entire young earth in ferment
from overflowing to overflowing —
        to remain a woman.

*Vanya Petkova*

## Full of You

That night when I held a light in the yard,
you were inside me
and the round-eyed earth flung open
its green arms
for us to make our way into it.
And somewhere constellations were exploding
and atomic invasions were shutting out
the rising sun with black berets.
And vanishing in a nemesis foretold
were the two-millenniums-old sources of Asia.
And somewhere the planet was bursting
like a small soap-bubble in the universe
in that night, when I held a light in the yard
and you were spurring your red horse
in my veins.
Full of you, I moved on
and carried all life in my cupped hands.
like water, for your parched lips,
and the trees in the night drew back
to the horizon, to let me pass.
It was a night to review and admire,
a weightless night of great beauty,
where every cell called out with the voice of a bird
that there was something more to this world.
And the wind conducted with a thousand batons
the rarest moment of my life.
In such a night it's not enough to just hold the light.
On such a night one should burn to death with a cry.

Vanya Petkova

# Sinner

Here — I'm a sinner.

I say what's in my mind,
I kiss what lips I choose,
and eyes the colour of a lake,
and eyes the colour of hazelnuts
I splash to the lees.

Here — I'm a sinner.

There are laws invented
to destroy me.
The sentences passed on me
weigh heavy on thousands of pages..

Eager arms outstretch
sinful fingers to my soul.
Profligate legs race
to grasp and crucify me.

Thousands of false suns
rise to blind me.
Wild streams of lava sweep
to melt and re-cast me.

Yet I remain a sinner
amidst the inimical cries
and after each sin
I write poetry.

*Vanya Petkova*

# Calling

Describe yourself in each verse,
paint yourself out like an icon
pecked by the beak of Time.
A crown of thorns awaits you
as reward, in recognition.
Are you worthy of one day winning such a prize?
Prettier after each suffering,
each time more replete
with harmony, with vibration and euphony.
You dominate yourself in such a way
that your short and insufficient life
is full of pain, but never dull.
You touched this world with nervous fingers,
shed flesh impatiently
from your unbuttoned blouse
to discover stalk after stalk in your way,
and you listened
to every breath, every pant, every sigh.
But there was an end and then nothing.
The crown of thorns still shines at the finish,
where, on its knees, the horizon
lifts that sack, full of star-corn
since the creation of the earth.
The crown of thorns awaits you —
the only golden aureole
worthy of your beautiful hair.
Are you worthy of one day winning such a prize?
Your life's so short
and every pleasure that's yours
delays your way to it.
Reach out your arms
to pass through the darkness
of this world like the blind
You, the richest on this earth,
with your crown of thorns.

Vanya Petkova

## At My Father's Grave

The ants and the sun mix
the black flour of the earth.
One lonely blade of grass
sways the colour of my eyes.
Carts creak
and sugar-sweet corn
rests in the cradle of my fingers.
I loved you so much.
No proof to show.
And the fact that I'm here
doesn't prove my love.
Nor the fact that I come
each day –
either.
I will be spying on the soil
which from now on
will harvest above you.
I will be spying every tiny stalk,
stem or flower.
I will wait for you
after the long journey
across stony ground and the mass of earth,
quartz, limestone and clay,
hydrogen, tender wet and brimstone.
I will wait for you
after the long journey
up here,
in order to recognize you.
And then
may my cry of joy
prove everything.
My fingers,
my lips, my knees...
My pain
and my joy
that you are with me once again.

# Other Bulgarian Titles Published by Forest Books

## STOLEN FIRE

Selected poems by Lyubomir Levchev
Translated by Ewald Osers

'Lyubomir Levchev has an easy way of talking, interrupted by bursts of humour. It is the relaxed talk of a man fully confident of himself and liking the world around him. There's something enormously healthy about him.' *(John Balaban)*

ISBN 0 948259 04 3          128pages/£5.95

## FIRES OF THE SUNFLOWER

Poems by Ivan Davidkov
Translated by Ewald Osers

Ivan Davidkov was a contemporary Bulgarian poet, prose writer and artist. His philosophical, lyrical poems make an urgent appeal to mankind to save the spiritual and material values which make life beautiful and meaningful.

ISBN 0 948259 48 5          96 pages/£6.95

## THE ROAD TO FREEDOM

Poems and Prose Poems by Geo Milev
Translated by Ewald Osers

This book contains perhaps the greatest epic poem of revolution in twentieth-century literature. Geo Milev's *September*, written to commemorate the uprising of Bulgarian workers and peasants in 1923 – regarded in Bulgaria as the first anti-fascist rising in Europe – is a poem of astonishing power, comparable to Shostakovich's recreation of Russia's October Revolution in his *Tenth Symphony*.

ISBN 0 948259 45 0          96 pages/£6.95

## POETS OF BULGARIA

Edited by William Meredith
Introduced by Alan Brownjohn

These Bulgarian poems should, and in these admirable translations they do, convey something new. Contact with this newness, with the courage and expansiveness, the lyrical freedom and the lurking alarm in the work of Luchesar Elenkov, Nikolai Hristozov, Boris Kristov and Lyubomir Levchev (to name only some), should be valuable and stimulating for English readers and poets, who are accustomed to powerful virtues of quite another kind in their own modern poetry.

ISBN 0 948259 39 6     106 pages/£6.95

## YOUNG POETS OF A NEW BULGARIA

Poems edited by Belin Tonchev
Introduced by Sebastian Barker

All the twenty-two poets in *Young Poets of a New Bulgaria* subscribe to what we might call a renewed vision of life. Nowhere else are we likely to see the youthful and unbroken face of Bulgaria more clearly than in this book. Whether in despair over politics, dreaming, unselfconscious, or falling in love, it is from amongst such faces the intellectual energy of the future will emerge to take up the challenge implicit in the failures of the past.

ISBN 0 948259 71 X     176 pages/£8.95